STORMPROOF

STORMPROOF

RECOVERY FROM COERCIVE CONTROL AND EMOTIONALLY ABUSIVE RELATIONSHIPS

PORTER QUINN

ISBN: 979-8-90221-202-7
Stormproof: Recovery from Coercive Control and Emotionally Abusive Relationships

May 2026

Published by Inner Peace Press
Eau Claire, Wisconsin, USA
www.innerpeacepress.com

Book promise

Whether you've been far too impacted by romantic love, an exploitative boss, a narcissistic family system, an abusive coach, or a controlling mentor, this book will show you what it cost you, how to use your own radar to avoid controlling relationships, how to stop carrying its logic forward into your new life so you never suffer this way again, and how to build a Stormproof life with less tolerance for weather that controls but calls itself care, ambition, family duty, team loyalty, or love.

Table of Contents

The Beacon

I wrote this book because, for decades, I have worked with people who left a controlling relationship, family, workplace, team, or mentorship and somehow felt worse afterward. Less sure of themselves. Less intact. Less able to explain what happened and the scale of the damage.

That confusion is not incidental. It is one of the injuries of coercive control.

Many people first learn about coercive control in romantic relationships. That is where it is most recognized, and where the language of love, rescue, devotion, and future can be most efficiently disguised. But coercive control does not belong to romance alone.

It can also take shape in a narcissistic family system, through a groomer's slow trust capture, under a caregiver engaging in factitious disorder imposed on another, or FDIA, in which a child's supposed illness or fragility becomes a route of control, beneath an exploitative boss, through a predatory mentor who converts guidance into ownership, inside a coercive coaching culture where discipline becomes domination and obedience is treated as character, or in cross-border and trafficker-like forms where movement, documents, legal vulnerability, and survival themselves become routes of leverage.

The setting changes. The logic does not.

In coercive control, a person or system downgrades your full humanity into yield. You are prized, recruited, studied, and drawn close. Then, over time, what was once treated as precious in you becomes something to manage, extract, diminish, or use. Your devotion, labor, steadiness, talent, credibility, body, loyalty, discipline, or conscience become part of somebody else's advantage. This is not a flaw in you. It reveals a cowardice in the person or system that is willing to convert another human being into a mere supply.

You may know it in your body before you can say it. Your days become less your own. Your instincts grow quieter. Your work, your rest, your privacy, your judgment, and your inner life begin getting rearranged around somebody else's weather.

This book is for you, the **Mark**.

I use that word on purpose. A Mark is not a fool. A Mark is a prize.

A Mark is selected for value, then eventually treated as disposable. A Mark is targeted because there is something worth taking: labor, beauty, steadiness, access, status, money, discipline, care, credibility, patience, usefulness, devotion, or reach. You are recruited, stripped for parts, degraded, and often later villainized for bearing the marks of what the system did to you.

From the outside, the arrangement may have looked like romance, family, mentorship, discipline, leadership, opportunity, team culture, or devotion. From the inside, it slowly became a private regime. One person's needs carried more weight. One person's version of events began crowding out reality. You, the Mark, were expected to adapt.

Coercive control is a cumulative pattern of domination in which one person uses demands, threats, surveillance, punishment, isolation, and manipulation of surrounding systems to entrap, degrade, and subordinate another person, reducing that person's autonomy, dignity, liberty, and everyday freedom.

That definition matters because coercive control often operates beneath the threshold that most people are trained to notice. Many professionals are still taught to look for isolated incidents, visible injury, overt force, or mutually framed conflict. Coercive control is invisible to most and is sometimes only indicated by the harm it causes.

Many victim-survivors of coercive control have also endured physical violence. Physical violence matters. It is not the sole measure of whether coercive control was real. A person can be hit, threatened, shoved, cornered, sexually pressured, restrained, terrorized by implication, or never physically struck at all, and still be living inside a regime of domination. Physical violence may be part of the system. It may also be unnecessary because surveillance, intimidation, financial erosion, humiliation, distortion, and consequence are already doing the work.

That is one reason so many survivors are misunderstood. They are asked whether there was hitting when the more accurate question is whether their life, judgment, movement, safety, and freedom were systematically invaded. This book exists to interrupt that invasion and its aftermath. This book has a companion website at CoerciveControlRecovery.com to support your clarity, growth, healing, community, and new chapter.

It is not your job to decide whether the Controller did all this knowingly, half-knowingly, opportunistically, or by reflex. What matters is impact. You do not need clearer evidence than your own erosion.

If your mind grew foggier, your body tighter, your time less yours, your work less stable, your standards less intact, your privacy negotiable, your money less free, your joy more expensive, or your self-trust harder to access, then something was happening.

We are going to name that something.

We are going to chart its system, assess its damage, and help you come out of it with your dignity more fully restored. We are here to move you toward a life harder to colonize.

A warning: You may need to hide this book.

If you are still near the Controller, still being watched, or still inside a system that punishes your clarity, keep this work private. Read it where your nervous system can hear itself. Let this book become a place where your experience can gather without interruption.

In a Stormproof life, privacy is not secrecy.

Privacy is a seawall.

You Are a Survivor

Many readers arrive here furious with themselves.

You may think you should have known sooner. That intelligence should have protected you. That goodness should have secured humane treatment. You may worry that your adaptation was proof of consent. You may hear the same old sneer rising in your own head: What was I thinking? How did I let this happen? Why didn't I leave earlier?

Stop.

You responded to coercive control while trying to stay afloat.

That is not the same thing as agreeing to it.

> *Coercive control performs an ugly trick. It creates overload, fear, dependence, distortion, humiliation, and consequences, then points to your adaptation as if it were the proof against you. It creates the rough sea, then mocks you for having a vessel in need of repair.*

This book will keep returning to a central correction:

Impact is not inadequacy. Adaptation is not consent.

If you are carrying the marks of coercive control, those marks do not prove that you were foolish, weak, dramatic, needy, or defective. They prove exposure. They prove a burden. They prove that your life encountered a system organized around your reduction.

Coercive control does not target people who would openly submit to domination from the start. It targets people with strengths worth using: loyalty, competence, intelligence, discipline, hope, patience, ambition, conscience, care, and the ability to keep trying. That is one reason the end of the relationship can feel so humiliating at first. Your best qualities were used to keep the system running.

What happened to you has a name. It has tactics. It has a structure. It leaves residue. Its impact often continues long after the relationship, role, household, team, or institution has changed.

That is why this book follows a clear voyage.

First, we name the system and break the Controller's illusion. Then we expose the extraction. Then we move into the aftermath: the Dirty Bombs, the Dead Zone, the injuries to personhood, body, and self-trust. From there, we move toward reclamation. We return reality to your own custody. We rebuild boundaries, standards, work, desire, and a sense of belonging. We build a life less available to occupation.

By the end, the Beacon will no longer sit outside you.

It will be yours.

Then you navigate by your own light.

The Book as a Beacon

A beacon cuts through fog.

You may already know something about beacons, even if you have not been using that word. A beacon may be the body signal you pushed through, thinking you should tough it out. The friend who would not be charmed into confusion by the Controller. The note, look, screenshot, or pattern you can no longer unknow. The small daily act that reminds you that your life is no longer under occupation.

A beacon tells the truth and keeps telling it.

That matters because coercive control gains influence by creating a fog of uncertainty. In fog, coercion is dressed as care. Surveillance is dressed as concern. Intrusion is dressed as love. Entitlement is dressed as guidance. Humiliation is dressed as discipline.

The beacon ends that arrangement.

It shows you the reef, the breach in the hull, and the way your own perception was pushed out of command.

> *Recovery from coercive control is not a single revelation. It is an ever-expanding transfer of authority back to the self.*

You have been living inside somebody else's rulebook, with shifting definitions of loyalty, safety, worth, service, and success. The method was the same regardless of setting: disable your instruments or discernment, contest your readings, replace your map, and call the takeover care.

This book is here to reverse that.

To help restore your instruments and discernment. To help return command. To help you become harder to capture in the same old weather.

Chapter One

The Toxic System You Were In

You may have thought you were dealing with a difficult relationship, a troubled household, a demanding boss, a complicated family, a charismatic mentor, a punishing coach, or a rough season that could be steadied by more patience. Many people do. It takes time to realize you were not only dealing with difficulty. You were living inside a system.

That system is coercive control.

Coercive control is a cumulative pattern of domination in which one person uses demands, threats, surveillance, punishment, isolation, and manipulation of surrounding systems to entrap, degrade, and subordinate another person, reducing that person's autonomy, dignity, liberty, and everyday freedom. It is most recognized in romance, but it does not belong solely to romance. It can organize a marriage, a family, a workplace, a mentorship, a coaching environment, a ministry, a team, or any hierarchy in which one person's power becomes more important than another person's humanity.

The point is not only to win arguments, secure compliance, or get one's way now and then. The point is to shape the conditions under which your life is lived until more of your time, judgment, movement, labor, privacy, and selfhood are organized around somebody else's power.

That is why the experience can be so hard to name at first. Many of the individual acts seem ordinary enough in isolation. A correction here. A private punishment. A favor that leaves you indebted. A revision of events that sends you back through your own memory as if the problem were your perception. A boss who keeps moving the standard. A mentor who calls intrusion guidance. A coach who treats obedience as character. A family system that mistakes your separateness for betrayal. What matters is the climate those acts create together. What matters is the way the whole arrangement begins to lean in one direction.

This book calls that territory the **Dead Zone**.

> *The Dead Zone is the psychological and practical environment in which coercive control takes hold deeply enough that it no longer needs constant spectacle or presence of the Controller to shape your life. Once you are living inside it, your preferences begin to meet friction, your separateness becomes costly, and your adaptation appears to outsiders as consent.*

You begin to edit yourself before anyone can correct you. You begin to anticipate a reaction before it arrives. You begin living around the weather.

That is one of the first injuries of coercive control. Your life stops feeling yours fully while remaining recognizable enough on the outside that others may not understand the cost. They may accidentally view the person controlling you as generous, well-meaning, and charismatic. People skilled at coercive control are masters of disguise.

The Dead Zone

Coercive control often enters under respectable cover. In romance, it may speak the language of love, partnership, rescue, devotion, protection, and future. In a family, it may speak the language of duty, respect, gratitude, closeness, or family traditions. In a workplace, it may come dressed as opportunity, standards, culture, access, or leadership. In mentorship, it may present as an unusual belief in your potential. In sport, it may speak the language of discipline, excellence, loyalty, and what it takes to win.

You feel chosen, seen, steadied, elevated, backed. Then the arrangement begins to tighten.

The Controller's comfort becomes a quiet organizing principle. Their priorities become urgent, central, and strangely self-explanatory. Your needs begin looking excessive, badly timed, selfish, confusing, expensive, or embarrassing. You are corrected into smaller accommodations. You do not knowingly sign onto that arrangement. You are trained in it.

That training often happens by consequence.

You pull away, and the temperature drops. You exercise independence, and the atmosphere hardens. You ask for reciprocity and find yourself in a swamp of denial, minimization, contempt, delay, defensiveness, or punishment. Relief becomes easier to secure than freedom. Compliance becomes cheaper than resistance. Over time, your system learns the lesson.

Nothing about that requires daily drama. A controlling system does not need a hurricane every morning. Drizzle will do. Enough friction, enough ambiguity, enough low-grade consequences, and ordinary life will reorganize itself around prevention. You become reluctant to want too much, say too much, remember too clearly, or refuse too firmly. What can I say? What do I want? What can I keep? What will this cost me later? Those questions begin to move underground and run your life from below.

> *That is why coercive control can feel sticky, disorienting, and hard to prove. Its deepest work is often done in the space between events. It is done in anticipation. It is done in self-editing. It is done in the narrowing of your range of motion. Worst of all, it often silently co-opts your own mind against you.*

That narrowing of your freedom matters. If you could no longer disagree without penalty, make plans without managing someone else's reaction first, protect your work without friction, keep private thoughts private, or remain fully yourself without paying for it later, then something structural was happening. It was not only stress. It was not only a conflict.

You were living in a private hierarchy.

Private Hierarchy

Coercive control is intimate, though it borrows an older social logic. One person becomes more central, more excusable, more interpretable as fully human. The other becomes more adjustable. The Controller gets greater latitude, more room to revise events, greater benefit of the doubt, and more authority over what counts. The Mark gets fewer allowances and more scrutiny. That is why the whole thing can feel faintly caste-like. The scale is smaller. The logic is familiar.

Unequal humanity gets normalized.

In a romantic bond, one partner becomes the weather while the other becomes the adapter. In a narcissistic family system, one parent or central figure becomes the axis around which everyone else organizes. In a workplace, the boss's version of reality may count more than the subordinate's lived experience. In an exploitative mentorship, the mentor's ambition, image, or access may quietly outrank the student's personhood. In a team setting, the coach's agenda may absorb the athlete's body, loyalty, and future while calling the arrangement character-building.

The Controller becomes contradictory, burdened, complicated, reactive, difficult, and misunderstood. The Mark gets read as needy, excessive, unstable, disloyal, dramatic, or hard to satisfy. The Controller's intentions carry weight. The Mark's impact is called into question. The Controller remains the axis around which interpretation turns. The Mark becomes increasingly legible as a function.

Once that structure settles in, many questions that torment survivors begin to answer themselves. Why did goodness not stabilize the bond? Why did fairness not prevail? Why did more effort fail to secure safety? Because systems of extraction are not corrected by giving them more valuable cargo.

The Controller and the Mark

The terms **Controller** and **Mark** help name the roles more cleanly.

The word **Controller** matters because the dynamic is organized around power over. The Controller may be magnetic, admired, spiritually literate, funny, accomplished, generous in public, wounded in self-story, or very convincing about why their harshness is necessary. They may be the beloved father, the charismatic founder, the star coach, the revered mentor, the partner everyone envies, the manager who "gets results." None of that changes the central fact. The relationship keeps reorganizing itself around their primacy. Their moods steer the ship. Their preferences set the terms. Their interpretations crowd the map.

Many Controllers would reject the label. Some think of themselves as noble, burdened, exacting for good reason, only trying to help, only responding to your inadequacy, ingratitude, disloyalty, or selfishness. Their self-story is rich in entitlement. That is one reason coercive control is so hard to explain. A person can be deeply committed to domination without using that word for themselves.

The word **Mark** matters because it corrects a common stigma. The target worries they are weak or stupid, but a Mark is not a fool. A Mark is a person selected precisely for their value.

Your value was targeted. You had something worth raiding and taking. Emotional steadiness. Reliability. Loyalty. Caretaking capacity. Attractiveness. Work ethic. Competence. Credibility. Housing. Income. Access. Patience. Conscience. The ability to keep trying. In romance, those traits may be harvested through attachment, dependency, domestic labor, sex, admiration, and hope. In families, they may be harvested through guilt, duty, over-functioning, and the wish to belong. In the workplace, they may be harvested through ambition, loyalty, and a hunger for opportunity. In coaching and mentorship, they may be cultivated through devotion, discipline, and a desire to become excellent under someone's guidance.

> *Those qualities are not evidence that you were weak.*
> *They are evidence that you were useful to someone who*
> *approached your humanity as yield.*

That is where dehumanization begins. Not when the treatment turns openly cruel. Earlier. Much earlier. The moment your full humanity stops acting as a limit in the Controller's mind, the downgrade is already underway. Your trust becomes access. Your labor becomes available. Your hope becomes a runway. Your attachment becomes leverage. Your dignity becomes negotiable if it stands in the way of advantage.

Many survivors spend years trying to repair that downgrade. They try to be fair enough, flexible enough, generous enough, accountable enough, loving enough that the relationship, the family, the team, the office, or the mentorship will return to the mutuality it promised at the start. That effort can deepen the trap because the Controller benefits from your conscience while remaining largely unfettered by one. Your best qualities begin working against you within the system. Your loyalty stabilizes it. Your hope extends it. Your discipline serves it. Your decency keeps giving it one more chance to become reciprocal.

The Long-Game Trap

What often keeps a person in the Dead Zone is not stupidity. It is the long game.

You tell yourself not to overreact. You tell yourself the relationship is under strain, the family is going through a phase, the boss is under pressure, the mentor is difficult but brilliant, the coach is hard because winning is hard. You tell yourself that children mature, companies stabilize, seasons pass, stress lifts, people soften, and the real relationship will finally have room to breathe. You think patience will be recognized as love, dedication, professionalism, loyalty, teachability, family devotion, or team spirit. You think steadiness will be met with steadiness. You think respect will slowly arrive if you do not force a crisis.

In a healthy system, time may soften things. In a coercive one, time is often used to train you.

One woman kept trying to take the long view in family life. The humiliations were small enough to dismiss one by one. Stepchildren corrected her tone, her laughter, her warmth, her very way of being in the home. Agreements were made and casually broken at her expense. She cooked, offered, adjusted, and kept hoping the atmosphere would improve if she stayed long enough to remain gracious. Each incident seemed too small to justify rupture. Each one also left the same residue: she was the one expected to absorb it. When she brought concerns to her partner, he minimized them, claimed not to notice, or treated the whole thing as beneath discussion. That refusal did more than avoid conflict. It set the tone. It told the room that her dignity was optional.

But the same trap appears elsewhere. The employee keeps telling himself the boss is demanding because the stakes are high and his contribution will eventually be recognized. The young professional keeps calling it mentorship because the mentor opened doors and must know best. The athlete keeps normalizing humiliation because elite environments are tough, and the coach is building greatness.

The adult child keeps shrinking because families are complicated, and maybe peace will come if she is just a little more understanding, a little less disruptive, a little easier to have around.

> *That is how the Dead Zone forms. Sometimes it arrives through spectacle. Often, it arrives through repeated diminishment that no authority interrupts. You begin by hoping to be accepted, promoted, selected, loved, trusted, or finally seen. You are often recruited by being made to feel exceptional. Then you become easier to correct, easier to bypass, easier to ignore.*

You stop wanting to make a big deal out of things because you believe restraint will eventually be rewarded. Instead, restraint becomes part of the machinery. The system learns that your hurt does not have to be addressed to keep your labor, loyalty, and presence.

The long game becomes even more dangerous once dependence is in place. Work has been reduced. Daily life has been reorganized. Practical exits are harder. A career path now runs through the boss. A future in the sport now runs through the coach. Family belonging feels tied to compliance. A relationship has become housing, identity, history, and hope. By then, the survivor is no longer only hoping for love or fairness. The Mark is hoping the sacrifice will eventually justify itself.

That is why hindsight can feel so degrading. The survivor looks back and thinks *I should have insisted on respect sooner, forced the issue earlier, and seen the truth before investing so much more.* The grief is real. It does not belong in the category of guilt. You were using normal relational logic in a system that was not organized around mutuality. You thought patience would be met with love, fairness, recognition, and a sense of earned belonging. Patience was converted into usable time.

A coercive system does not leave dignity unprotected because it has forgotten. It leaves dignity unprotected because accountability interferes with advantage. Respect would require restraint, effort, and a willingness to limit one's own convenience. The Dead Zone does not prefer that kind of friction. It prefers the easier arrangement: your discomfort privately absorbed, your hope still active, your place in the system still intact enough to be useful.

If your dignity keeps being deferred to some later season, the delay carries information. The delay is not neutral. The delay is the mechanism.

How the Controller Wins

> The Controller is rarely a roaring tyrant. Some are soft-spoken. Some are self-effacing. Many are well regarded. Many prefer the undertow of the Dead Zone to do their work. They win through engineered rescue, selective favor, ambiguity, triangulation, delay, reputation handling, information control, and quiet rearrangement.

In one setting, the Controller is a partner who audits your time, rewrites events, and punishes distance. In another, a parent who rewards enmeshment and punishes separation. Elsewhere, a boss offers special access, then extracts more and restricts opportunity when you push back. Elsewhere, a mentor who calls entitlement guidance and dependence gratitude. Elsewhere, a coach who grants favor, moves the line, and dresses obedience up as devotion.

The surfaces change. The current does not.

Example: The Helpful Captor

At first, Roger's help seemed competent. He moved quickly, solved problems fast, and always seemed to have a better way of doing things. Laurel resisted in the beginning. She had run her own freelance business for years and did not need improvement. Over time, resistance grew tiring. He could do it faster. He could do it better. He would take over, then remind her of the fact that he had taken over.

Eventually, he turned his attention to her career.

Since he earned more, he argued that her work was distracting them from their future. It made more sense, he said, for her to support his career and let him cover expenses. The arrangement sounded practical. His career surged. Their daily life revolved around his accumulation.

He said he could never have done it without her. She was meant to take that as a sign of gratitude.

Her body was taking in a different truth. She felt listless, less competent, less like herself. She stopped seeing friends because he framed them as a distraction. She gained weight. She became more dependent on the man who had helped create the conditions of that dependence. Years later, he discarded her, called her a burden, and refused meaningful support while she tried to rebuild work, health, and safety from the wreckage of a life that had been organized around him.

> *Laurel's humiliation was not only heartbreak. It was the shock of realizing that the dependence he later despised was the very dependence he had engineered.*

The same structure appears outside romance. A boss "develops" you until your ideas, labor, and loyalty are baked into his or her advancement. A mentor "launches" you while making your future increasingly conditional on pleasing him. A coach becomes the route to your goals, then acts as though your body, time, and obedience belong to the program. A narcissistic family system recruits the most conscientious member to absorb strain, preserve appearances, and keep everyone else comfortable. Different titles and costumes. Same mechanism.

What you measure matters. That's why I developed the CoerciveControlRecovery.com website as a companion for this book. There, you can take the following screen if you wish, or simply score it here on paper. Either way, witnessing your own assessment of the erosion caused by coercive control in the landscape of your life is an act of reclamation and helps protect you against further exploitation.

A Brief Screen

Are/Were You Living Under Coercive Control or Emotional Abuse?

By the time many people begin to suspect coercive control, they are already arguing with themselves.

Maybe it was only stress, a difficult season, or miscommunication. Maybe the bond was intense, but real. Maybe the family was just complicated. Maybe the price of staying close was simply higher than expected. Maybe the confusion was mine.

That is one reason a brief screen can help. It gives the mind somewhere firmer to stand.

The most important question is not only what the Controller did, but how it impacted your life. What did the system do to you? What happened to your range? Your self-trust? Body? Work? Privacy? Money? Your sense that your life was still fully yours?

Use the questions below as a pattern-recognition tool.

Instructions

Rate each statement from **1 to 5**.
1 = **not at all**
2 = **a little**
3 = **neutral, mixed, or sometimes**
4 = **quite a bit**
5 = **severe, frequent, or very true**

Screening Questions

1. I feel I must monitor this person's mood, tone, or reactions to stay safe or avoid fallout.

2. I have become more careful about what I say because honesty or disagreement often backfires.

3. I felt unusually chosen, special, or deeply attached early on, in a way that quickly built trust.

4. I have stayed invested because of promises, future plans, or hoped-for change that never fully arrived.

5. I feel pressure to explain myself in situations where my privacy or autonomy should simply be respected.

6. I have felt responsible for keeping the peace, stabilizing the relationship, or preventing things from getting worse.

7. I second-guess my memory, judgment, or interpretation after conversations with this person.

8. I feel my world has grown smaller because this person has limited my contact, attention, or access to other people, perspectives, or sources of support.

9. I feel my time is less my own and is increasingly organized around this person's needs, demands, or reactions.

10. I feel my movement, travel, routines, or plans are more constrained than they should be.

11. I feel that documents, passwords, reservations, accounts, residency status, citizenship help, legal standing, or even my passport have been used to increase my dependence or reduce my freedom.

12. I have made important decisions based on fear of what will happen if I refuse, leave, expose, or disappoint them.

13. I have experienced humiliation, contempt, ridicule, or quiet put-downs that made me feel smaller.

14. I have felt ashamed in ways that seem bigger than what I did wrong.

15. I feel my body has changed under this stress through sleep problems, dread, numbness, exhaustion, appetite changes, or feeling on edge.

16. I have felt emotionally pulled back toward this person even after recognizing harmful patterns.

17. I have felt punished through withdrawal, silence, coldness, exclusion, or loss of approval when I became more separate.

18. I feel I am expected to follow small rules, rituals, or demands that may seem minor on their own but together make me feel watched, managed, or worn down.

19. I worry that this person could damage my reputation, work, finances, custody, legal standing, or future if I resist them.

20. I feel my life has become narrower, harder to inhabit, or less fully mine.

Scoring

Please add your responses to get a **total score out of 100**.

20 to 39

Lower pattern endorsement. That does not erase harm. Some coercive systems are intermittent, newly forming, or concentrated in only a few areas.

40 to 59

Mild to moderate concern. Some coercive or emotionally abusive dynamics may be present and deserve closer attention.

60 to 79

Strong concern. The pattern may be affecting your self-trust, daily freedom, body, or functioning in meaningful ways.

80 to 100

High concern. The pattern is likely severe, pervasive, or life-shaping.

Red-Flag Override

Regardless of total score, pay special attention if you rated **4 or 5** on items **1, 7, 8, 11, 12, 15, 19, or 20**. Those items often point to fear, reality distortion, isolation, dependency through movement or legal status, bodily impact, practical leverage, and narrowing of life.

A Final Note

No brief screen can tell the whole story. Coercive control accumulates. It spreads. It often hides in ordinary-looking arrangements until your life is already being organized around somebody else's power.

If your score stirred recognition, do not get stuck asking whether every incident was dramatic enough. Ask the more faithful question: what has this system done to your life?

For readers who want more context-specific screens, see *Appendix A*, which includes additional quizzes for professional control, athletic coaching, coercive family systems, and predatory trust capture.

The Toxic System You Were In

If you take only one thing from this chapter, let it be this: what happened to you was not a random misfortune and not simply bad communication. You were living in a system that narrowed your life while training you to explain the narrowing away.

Once that becomes clear, many old questions lose their grip. Why didn't devotion stabilize it? Why didn't fairness rescue it? Why didn't professionalism, loyalty, discipline, or family love finally secure humane treatment? Those questions belong to mutual systems. Coercive control is organized around rank, yield, and consequence. It is not corrected by your goodness.

> *Recovery begins when you stop asking what hidden moral formula would have made the Dead Zone humane and start asking more protective questions. What is the system? How did it work? What did it cost? What would keep it from reinstalling itself? How do I build a life less available to occupation?*

Those are the right questions.

Those are the questions that begin to return the helm to you.

Chapter Two
How Coercive Control Works

By the time most people can name coercive control, they have already spent too long trying to explain it one incident at a time.

A strange text. A correction. A favor with strings. A moving target. A withheld opportunity. A family scene that leaves you ashamed. A workplace humiliation that somehow gets framed as your growth opportunity. A coach's demand that sounds like discipline until you notice your own humanity no longer acts as a limit. A mentor's special attention starts to feel more like possession than guidance. A partner's care that quietly becomes governance.

On their own, many of these moments can still be argued with. Together, they reveal a structure.

> *Coercive control is not a pile of bad moments. It is an operating system. It does not rely on one tactic. It works by combining tactics until the target's reality, freedom, dignity, and room to move are steadily reduced. That is why it can feel so hard to describe.*

You are not dealing with one problem. You are dealing with a system that keeps changing costumes while preserving the same objective.

This chapter names that system more plainly.

I use three organizing frameworks here:

- **EXTRACT**, which describes how coercive control operates
- **CONS**, which describes the inner drivers that fuel it
- **SEIZES**, which describes what the system does to the target over time

Do not worry about memorizing them all at once. Their purpose is simpler than that. They are here to help you stop arguing with the weather and start reading the climate.

EXTRACT

The EXTRACT system (see pages 29-30) names the recurring architecture of coercive control. Whether the setting is romance, family, work, mentorship, or sport, the same pattern tends to appear. It helps you stop treating coercive acts as unrelated incidents and start seeing them as moves in a system with a motive.

E: Ensnarement

Coercive control rarely begins with an obvious demand to surrender your life. It begins with pull.

You are drawn in through specialness, urgency, intensity, recognition, unusual promise, relief, or concern. In romance, you may feel unusually chosen, unusually understood, unusually safe. In family life, belonging may be offered on terms that initially feel close rather than colonizing. At work, a boss may single you out as exceptional. A mentor may claim to see something rare in you. A coach may tell you that you have what it takes. The form changes. The seduction stays the same.

> *Ensnarement feels meaningful because it imitates genuine recognition. The Controller mirrors your values, your hopes, your language, your goals, or your hunger for something missing. Private access opens before trust has been earned.*

The connection moves faster than good judgment would prefer, but the speed gets sold as chemistry, rescue, loyalty, ambition, family, or fate.

That acceleration matters.

Before your appraisal is complete, the Controller has already gained privileged access to your life.

X: eXploitation

Once you are inside the system, what is yours no longer remains fully yours.

Your time becomes flexible in one direction. Your emotional steadiness becomes a resource. Your labor and talent become easier to assume than to request. Your privacy becomes offensive. Your goodwill becomes a hiding place for someone else's entitlement.

In romance, this may look like your schedule becoming more interruptible, your body more available, your care more expected, your future more rearranged around the bond. In a family, it may look like one person's distress becomes everybody else's staffing plan.

> *At work, your competence becomes infrastructure for someone else's rise. In mentorship, your devotion becomes something to harvest. In sport, your body may be treated as an asset to be spent.*

Competent people often minimize exploitation because contribution is familiar to them. They are used to being strong, useful, and generous. That is one reason coercive systems so often recruit capable people. Capability conceals the theft for a while.

T: Tension Cultivation

The Controller does not need daily chaos. A charged atmosphere will do.

A look that makes you check yourself. A silence that raises anxiety. A question with a test hidden inside it. A coolness after you act independently. A manager who goes vague when you need clarity. A mentor who grows distant when you show self-direction. A parent who punishes separateness with disappointment. A coach whose approval has become strangely expensive.

The point is not random moodiness. The point is conditioning.

> *Tension teaches you to anticipate fallout. You start stabilizing the weather before it breaks. You monitor tone, timing, language, posture, access, and reaction. Your nervous system gets trained to swing between vigilance and numbness. The Controller no longer must be in the room all the time. The climate of the Dead Zone is doing the work.*

R: Reality Distortion and Reputation Control

Reality theft is one of the central injuries of coercive control because so much else depends on it.

Events get revised. Motives get assigned to you. Your reading gets treated as suspect. The thing you clearly saw becomes the thing you must now debate. You are told what happened, what you meant, what others think, what no one reasonable would conclude, and what matters more than what actually hurt you.

At the same time, the Controller may begin managing your reputation. This can happen subtly. A sarcastic comment. A preemptive story. This portrait depicts you as unstable, demanding, disloyal, dishonest, difficult, overly sensitive, not team-oriented, insufficiently grateful, and emotionally immature. In romance, this may happen with friends or family. In family systems, it occurs through roles such as the scapegoat or the golden child. In workplaces, it happens in rooms you are not in. In coaching and mentorship, it can determine who is believed before you ever speak.

> *Reality distortion not only confuses you. It influences the social field around you. It steals time. It forces you to spend energy defending the basic integrity of your own map.*

A: Access Control

Coercive control depends on too much reach.

Under the guise of care, concern, duty, mentorship, leadership, or closeness, the Controller gains increasing access to territories that should remain under your custody. Your schedule. Your whereabouts. Your devices. Your body. Your work. Your social life. Your emotional availability. Your money. Your privacy. Your rest.

> *Access control is not only surveillance. It can sound like commentary, assumption, interruption, management, checking, insistence, expectation, and informal ownership. It can look like your calendar is being filled faster than you can name your priorities for your time.*

Once access expands, autonomy begins getting renamed. Privacy becomes secrecy. A boundary becomes selfishness. Distance becomes betrayal. Time for your own interests becomes disloyalty. A separate judgment becomes disrespectful. You then spend energy defending what should have remained yours without argument.

C: Coercion by Consequence

Coercive systems often prefer consequences to direct command because consequences leave less evidence and train the target more efficiently.

You resist, delay, question, withdraw, disagree, choose for yourself, or simply remain fully separate, and the atmosphere shifts. Belonging becomes unstable. Opportunity narrows. The next hours, days, or weeks get harder than they needed to be.

> *You learn that resistance is expensive. Compliance is cheaper. Sometimes it even feels safer.*

In romance, this may mean distance, contempt, sulking, punishment, surveillance, or financial pressure. In family life, it may mean guilt, exclusion, disapproval, or a role shift against you. At work, it may mean lost access, diminished support, stalled advancement, or quiet sidelining. In mentorship, it may mean withdrawal of favor. In sport, it may mean less play, more humiliation, or reputational downgrading disguised as correction.

That is coercion by consequence. Nothing must be formally ordered. The lesson still lands.

T: Traps

Traps turn ordinary life into a minefield.

These include double binds, no-win tests, baited questions, false choices, moving standards, goal-post shifts, hidden meanings attached to ordinary decisions, and offers that later become debts. Your need for time, privacy, sleep, due process, healing, money, or dignity is recast as a defect, defiance, manipulation, weakness, selfishness, or a lack of character.

In a coercive family, this may look like being punished whether you comply or separate. At work, it may look like being criticized for both initiative and restraint. In a mentoring relationship, it may look like being told to think independently, only to be punished when you do. In romance, it may look like being asked for honesty, then penalized for the truth. In sport, it may look like being told toughness matters most, until your limits interfere with someone else's agenda.

> *Traps are effective because they corrode confidence. Once ordinary life keeps producing hidden costs, you begin hesitating before taking up any space at all.*

Taken Together

Ensnarement pulls you close before the situation is fully appraised.

e**X**ploitation converts your gifts into expected supply.

Tension keeps your system over-responsive or numb.

Reality distortion fogs the compass.

Access control expands informal ownership over your life.

Coercion by consequence trains behavior through penalty.

Traps make ordinary existence harder to inhabit.

That is **EXTRACT**.

It is the architecture of coercive control.

Coercive control does not belong to romance alone. The setting changes. The governing logic does not. The chart on the following pages outlines the system at work across different contexts.

EXTRACT Across Contexts:
Different Controllers, Same System

Type	Ensnarement	eXploitation	Tension
Romantic Controller	love, rescue, future	sex, labor, admiration	jealousy, withdrawal
Cross-border controller	relocation, rescue, shared future	dependence, assets, legal vulnerability	isolation, uncertainty
Narcissistic family system	belonging, duty	caretaking, silence	scapegoating, favoritism
Groomer	specialness, secrecy	body, loyalty, silence	boundary testing
Munchausen / FDIA caregiver*	caregiving, alarm	body, fear, dependency	crises, uncertainty
Exploitative boss	praise, opportunity	ideas, labor, loyalty	ambiguity, delay
Predatory mentor	special recognition	devotion, orbit	unstable favor
Coercive coach	elite promise	body, discipline	humiliation, unstable approval
Trafficker / captor	rescue, shelter	body, labor, survival	threat, scarcity

EXTRACT Across Contexts:
Different Controllers, Same System

Reality distortion	Access	Consequence	Traps
gaslighting, DARVO	time, body, money	contempt, exile	loyalty tests
lies about laws, rights, intentions	movement, documents, residency	jurisdictional disadvantage, immigration fear, asset leverage	relocation framed as love, safety, or opportunity
family myth	privacy, time	guilt, exclusion	double binds
normalization, confusion	private contact	shame, silence	complicity traps
false illness story	records, appointments	fear, isolation	independence framed as danger
reputation harm, revision	time, availability	retaliation	moving standards
control framed as guidance	schedule, future	withdrawal of favor	autonomy punished
harm framed as toughness	training, body	exclusion, status loss	limits framed as weakness
lies about options	documents, movement	violence, deprivation	fake choices

* A caregiver who uses a child's supposed illness, fragility, or medical crisis as a route of control. In factitious disorder imposed on another (FDIA), the caregiver may exaggerate, fabricate, or induce symptoms, then build identity, attention, and authority around the child's dependency and fear.

CONS

If EXTRACT names how the system operates, **CONS** names what fuels it.

Many survivors spend years studying the behavior on their own. The texts, the punishments, the charm, the reversals, the humiliations, the false rescues, the no-win tests. That study matters. But it can leave an important question unanswered: what kind of inner machinery keeps generating this weather in the first place?

CONS is not a diagnostic tool. It is a way of naming the psychological forces that often drive the coercive system.

C: Cowardice

> *Cowardice is the first wall of the Dead Zone.*
>
> *A fair fight would require the Controller to stand in ordinary human proportion. It would require them to risk being known, corrected, disappointed, limited, or refused. Cowardice does not want that kind of exposure. It wants an advantage without an equal encounter.*

Leverage.

That is why coercive control so often comes at you sideways.

Cowardice hides inside charm, ambiguity, selective tenderness, concern, spiritual language, leadership language, family language, or the posture of burden. It avoids direct truth when doing so would cost power. It prefers veiled threats, passive aggression, strategic confusion, distortion, reputation management, character assassination, and consequence over clean accountability.

The asymmetry becomes familiar. The Controller has strong reactions and weak ownership. Grand language about love, mission, family, standards, excellence, or sacrifice, with very little willingness to submit the self to the obligations those words would impose.

Cowardice builds the walls because it fears your clarity and will not risk mutual transparency.

O: Obsessive Compulsiveness

This is not a clinical diagnosis here. It is a way of naming the patterned drive to regulate the whole map.

Obsessive compulsiveness in coercive control means the Controller keeps trying to manage the environment, the narrative, your options, your timing, your movement, your relationships, your access, your routines, your availability, and your independent centers of gravity.

> *Cowardice builds the perimeter. Obsessive compulsiveness curates the interior.*

Life starts feeling like a maze. Rules multiply. Tiny deviations carry too much charge. Your spontaneity irritates the system. Your body, your phone, your work, your evenings, your lunch hour, your privacy, your friendships, and your travel all begin feeling less fully yours.

The point is not tidiness. The point is governability.

N: Narcissistic Fragility

Narcissistic fragility is the vortex that cannot tolerate your separateness for long.

A myth of popular psychology is that narcissism masks low self-worth or shame. But research confirms that narcissistic cruelty is fed by a sense of entitlement. The cruelty is not reactive. The cruelty is calculated domination and exploitation. What appears at first to be benevolence is a presentation conditional on admiration. The performance of benevolence dissolves once superiority is threatened. Charm or seduction is replaced with degradation, contempt, belittlement, and even rage, deployed to continue the exploitation and destabilization of the Mark to maintain structural dominance, because relationships are viewed as hierarchical, not reciprocal.

The flow of admiration and submission within the relationship must be managed. Once a Mark is seduced into an arrangement, the very "no" that had commanded a resemblance of respect or excitement in the Controller is interpreted as betrayal.

> *Any threat to image – even as simple as perceived criticism, loss of admiration, or fear of exposure – justifies disproportionate, aggressive countermeasures against the Mark. Deliberate campaigns of humiliation, invalidation, and covert relational aggression are fair game to the Controller against the Mark.*

The very qualities that first made you desirable to the Controller later become threatening. Your competence. Your joy. Your success. Your clarity. Your boundaries. Your independent thought. Your recovery. Your refusal to revolve around them. These things destabilize a self that depends on centrality.

So, the system punishes growth.

In romance, this may look like criticism, jealousy, reinterpretation, or contempt when you become more solid. In family systems, it may look like withdrawal or scapegoating when you differentiate. At work, it may look like devaluation the moment you seek authorship, autonomy, or recognition. In mentorship, it may look like hostility when you stop idealizing the guide. In sport, it may look like punishment for having a body, a boundary, or an identity that exceeds the role assigned to you.

Narcissistic fragility wants everything orbiting the Controller's equilibrium. Your full life becomes a problem when it no longer feeds that center.

S: Sadism

Sadism is the quiet relief the Controller experiences as you shrink.

This does not always look like theatrical cruelty. Often, it is subtler, making it more deniable and chilling. The Controller seems calmer when you are less alive, less separate, less confident, less demanding of reciprocal humanity. Your confusion soothes them.

> *Your diminishment stabilizes them. Your self-doubt increases the room they occupy to move.*
>
> *That is why pain is not a deterrent in coercive systems. Sometimes your pain is part of how the system regulates itself.*

This helps explain why repair so often fails to arrive, even when the Controller understands your hurt well enough. Understanding is not the same as conscience. In some systems, your diminishment is not a side effect. It is part of the payoff.

Taken Together

Cowardice builds the walls.
Obsessive compulsiveness builds the maze.
Narcissistic fragility pulls everything toward its center.
Sadism takes relief in your erosion.

That combination creates the Dead Zone.

Once you see that, you stop treating coercive control as a string of isolated incidents and begin seeing it as a psychological ecosystem organized around your reduction.

SEIZES

If CONS names the inner drivers, EXTRACT names the architecture, and **SEIZES** names what the system does to the target over time.

It erodes. It isolates. It zones in on strengths. It steers you away from clarity.

S: Shapes Reality, Seduces Trust, Subjugates

The Controller presents a front designed to attract your trust.

Fairness. Transparency. Rescue. Guidance. Care. Opportunity. Loyalty. Vision. Family. Safety. Excellence. Their persona is built to lower your guard. Trust is not seized all at once. It is invited forward. Then the relationship changes speed.

> *Subjugation rarely announces itself. It arrives through shifting terms. Their perspective becomes more structurally important. Your "no" becomes harder to hold. Your own center gives way under the pressure of someone else's self-story.*

In romance, this can look like rescue becoming rule. In work, sponsorship becomes ownership. In mentorship, guidance becomes a claim. In coaching, belief becomes control. In family systems, closeness becomes enmeshment and fusion.

E: Erodes Identity, Engenders Dependence, Expands Control

Once trust is seduced, erosion follows.

You lose touch with your own preferences, standards, rhythms, and range of motion. Dependence is induced through practical, emotional, narrative, and sometimes financial means. The system becomes more central to your identity, future, and permission to move.

As dependence deepens, control expands.

You may still feel as though you are making choices. Often you are. But the field in which those choices occur has been narrowed. That narrowing is one of the system's quietest victories.

I: Isolates, Intimidates, Intensifies

The system cuts you off from alternative reality checks.

Old friends look suspicious. Outside input looks contaminated. Independent time looks disloyal. Outside support looks threatening to the bond, the family, the team, or the mission. Intimidation may be overt or quiet. It may come through looming, silence, sarcasm, exclusion, strategic withdrawal, contempt, humiliation, or the simple knowledge that noncompliance will cost you.

Then the intensity increases.

False crises appear. The emotional pressure rises. Your nervous system becomes organized around management rather than ordinary living.

> *Isolation makes you easier to govern. Intimidation makes you easier to steer. Intensity makes appraisal harder.*

Z: Zones in on Strengths

Controllers do not target you because you are weak.

They zone in on strengths for their own purposes.

Your steadiness. Your loyalty. Your discernment. Your discipline. Your social credibility. Your ability to absorb stress. Your hunger to do good work. Your wish to love well. Your wish to belong honorably. Your ability to read a room. Your willingness to persevere.

Then those strengths are converted.

Your work ethic becomes indentured servitude. Your emotional maturity becomes the system's shock absorber. Your devotion becomes leverage. Your talent becomes someone else's asset. Your patience and loyalty become a hiding place for their delays and distortions.

> *That is why coercive control wounds so deeply. What was best in you was not cherished as yours. It was studied for yield.*

E: Enmeshment and Emotional Enslavement

At this stage, boundaries become hard to locate.

> *Your identity begins blurring under the weight of someone else's moods, agendas, and stories. You find yourself managing their weather from inside your own body.*

On the surface, you may still appear professional, teachable, loving, or composed. Inwardly, more of the self is being requisitioned day by day into the system. That is why many survivors say they disappeared while still functioning.

The self was not gone. It was no longer fully in charge.

S: Steers You Away from Your Beacon

The final move is strategic disorientation.

The Controller takes the helm and turns you away from what would increase clarity. Your body's warnings. Outside witnesses. Unbiased feedback. Your own future. Your own life.

> *The farther you are steered from Beacon, the easier the Dead Zone is to mistake for ordinary water.*
>
> *That is the point.*

False Beacons

Once you understand EXTRACT, CONS, and SEIZES, a few recurring deceptions become easier to see. I call these false beacons because they appear to offer guidance while drawing you deeper into the regime.

Engineered Rescue

Something is difficult. You are tired, threatened, pressured, uncertain, in grief, under family strain, financially stretched, professionally vulnerable, or longing for recognition. Then someone arrives with decisive help, protection, guidance, contacts, or unusual belief in you.

The calm feels real. The relief may even be real. The problem is what the help becomes.

> *Real help restores your footing and returns you to yourself. Engineered rescue binds relief to authority. It makes the Controller seem necessary before trust has been earned.*

Gratitude starts turning into indebtedness. Dependence becomes evidence that they should keep the helm.

This happens in romance all the time. It also happens with bosses who "take you under their wing," mentors who "open doors," family members who overhelp, and coaches who treat their support as ownership over your future.

Engineered rescue is one of the cleanest ways that coercive control gains a lawful-looking entry into your life. It rarely arrives wearing domination on its face. It arrives looking useful, and stabilizing. Only later do you discover the rescue had a second function: it was also a route of colonization.

Future Faking

Future faking works by keeping you oriented toward what is about to happen rather than what is happening now.

The commitment that never settles. The promotion that never lands or arrives in a diminished form. The repair is always around the corner. The family peace that will come once this season passes. The role you are promised if you stay loyal. The reward that moves just ahead of the pain.

The form changes. The structure stays the same.

> *Something important is kept near enough to organize your sacrifice, loyalty, and ambition, but never fully delivered.*

> *Future faking is bait by horizon.*

False Empowerment

False empowerment is staged authority.

The Mark is made to feel chosen, trusted, elevated, influential, and essential. Yet the real authority remains elsewhere. Your power is welcome only so long as it serves the regime. The moment you reach for real independence, or real authorship, the weather changes.

This is common in exploitative workplaces, mentorships, and coaching environments, though it also appears in romance and family life.

> *You are made to feel special inside a structure that remains fundamentally unequal.*

> *That is the tell.*

What was offered was not sovereignty. It was a staged agency.

What This Chapter Is Here to Do

This chapter is not asking you to become a perfect diagnostician of everyone who has ever held power over you. It is asking for something more useful.

It is asking you to stop misreading the weather as random.

> *Once the system becomes visible, your experience begins to organize itself differently. The humiliation stops looking mysterious. The delay stops looking neutral. The self-blame loses some of its power. You begin to see structure where you once saw confusion.*

That matters because recovery begins there. You do not need to solve the Controller. You need to recognize the system.

Once you can do that, the next questions become possible. What did it cost? What was stolen? What residue did it leave behind? How do you return to your own custody?

Those are the questions that move you toward open water.

Chapter Three

Tactics of the Controller and the Hidden Costs

By the time coercive control starts making sense, many people are already asking the wrong question.

They ask: Why am I still so affected by something that so few noticed from the outside?

That question makes sense. It also gives too much credit to appearances.

> *Coercive control rarely relies on one giant event. It gets leverage through accumulation. A humiliation here. A delayed or withheld apology there.*

A threat that never has to fully land because the implication already did the work. A private correction. A public downgrade. A broken promise that somehow becomes your confusion. A role you did not mean to occupy becomes the terms of your life.

The Controller does not need every tactic in every setting. A romantic exploiter, a narcissistic family system, an exploitative boss, a possessive mentor, and a coercive coach may use different combinations. The underlying objective stays the same: reduce your range of motion, increase your self-doubt, make your labor and loyalty easier to claim, and keep your reality expensive to defend.

This chapter names some of the most common tactics and the hidden costs they leave behind.

Dirty Bombs and Hidden Cost

A controlling system often remains active through a sticky web of residue.

That residue is what I call a **Dirty Bomb**.

A Dirty Bomb is fallout planted inside you by coercive control. It is the part that keeps going off after the obvious moment has passed. It is the afterlife of the regime in the mind and body. The sentence you cannot stop hearing. The spike of shame that arrives before thought. The panic over an ordinary choice or seemingly small transition. The bodily dread that appears before your conscious mind names the trigger. The compulsion to explain. The loop in which you keep trying to prove your case to a person or system already committed to denying and distorting it.

> *Dirty Bombs do not only operate during the relationship, the family role, the job, the mentorship, or the season with the coach. They are designed to keep detonating after the visible structure has already cracked.*

That is why so many survivors feel most confused after the system has already broken open. They expect lower contact, legal boundaries, a job exit, a breakup, graduation, a move, or geographic separation to bring peace. Sometimes there is relief. There is often fallout, too. Dirty Bombs keep the mind trying to navigate through a sea that was never going to become safe.

Pirate's Poison: Common Dirty Bombs

Carried Shame

One of the Controller's most efficient achievements is to leave you carrying the moral weight of what they did.

Instead of landing cleanly on the fact that you were lied to, used, manipulated, overruled, humiliated, or exposed to a system organized around your diminishment, your mind turns inward and starts writing an indictment against you.

You should have known.
You should have left sooner.
You were weak.
You were pathetic.
You allowed it.
You betrayed yourself.

That is carried shame.

The shame feels real. Its assignment is false. You carry a burden that belongs elsewhere.

> *The Controller extracted your valuable resources without naming the cost, and you are left combing your past for what is supposedly wrong with you.*

In romance, that shame may attach to love, sex, money, or overstaying. In family systems, it may attach to loyalty, distance, anger, or the wish to belong. At work, it may attach to ambition, deference, professional hope, or silence. In coaching and mentorship, it may be attached to wanting approval, specialness, advancement, or protection.

Carried shame works because it turns a structural injury into a private flaw. Carried shame decreases with community and better information. These are also available to you on CoerciveControlRecovery.com.

Internalized Ranking

Even after direct contact ends, the old grading system may remain active inside you.

You still hear the Controller's scale. How you speak. What you spend. How you dress. Whether you are productive enough, strong enough, reasonable enough, attractive enough, loyal enough, grateful enough, impressive enough, or team-oriented enough.

In a narcissistic family system, this voice may sound like old duty. In a workplace, it may sound like perform better, complain less, and prove more. In coaching, it may sound like tougher, leaner, more obedient. In romance, it may sound like smaller, quieter, and easier to love.

That is one of coercive control's grimmest efficiencies.

> *Coercive control outsources monitoring into your own mind.*

Fear and Hypervigilance

You keep scanning because scanning once protected you.

Details of a story that don't match your lived reality. Texts. Tone. Doors. Footsteps. Calendars. Financial movements. Legal messages. Facial expressions. Silences. Delays. Praise. Withholding. The tiny shifts that used to mean the weather was coming. An elevated startle response.

From the outside, this can look exaggerated. From the inside, it is learned survival.

> *Hypervigilance occurs when the cost of missing a signal is too high for too long.*

Accountability Avoidance and Reversal

Among the many tactics Controllers use, one of the clearest has been named by psychologist Jennifer Freyd: **DARVO**, which stands for **Deny, Attack, Reverse Victim and Offender**.

This is the move in which the person who caused harm denies it, attacks the person who named it, and then claims the position of the injured person.

> *You raise a concern. They become the one mistreated by your tone, your timing, your ingratitude, your suspicion, your instability, your betrayal, your failure to understand. Suddenly, your effort to name harm has been turned into evidence against you.*

Controllers use this move in romance, family disputes, offices, legal settings, and coaching cultures because it does three jobs at once: it evades accountability, destabilizes your confidence, and repositions power.

Manufactured Kindness and Love Bombing

There is often a rush to intensity that should have taken more time for genuine mutuality.

Flattery. Heroic protectiveness. Specialness. Future faking language. Surprising generosity. Strong language about destiny, calling, family, greatness, once-in-a-lifetime connection, unusual faith in your ability, unusual safety in their presence. These gestures may contain real energy. They are also useful to a controlling system because they move trust forward faster than careful appraisal would.

> *What makes the kindness manufactured is not that every kind act was fake. It is that kindness serves control more than conscience. It opens the lane. It disarms. It secures access.*

It creates a story you will later use against your own clarity.

Trauma Bonding

Trauma bonding occurs when attachment is braided with fear, intermittent relief, and consequences. Intermittent reinforcement fuels addictive and impulsive behavior. It makes you feel desperate and is demoralizing.

The person or system that hurts you also provides moments of warmth, recognition, or relief that ease the hurt. That creates terrible confusion. Longing strengthens in the very place where clarity should be easiest. A family system wounds you, then briefly lets you back in. The boss humiliates you, then singles you out for praise. The partner withdraws, then returns just enough warmth to reopen hope. The coach punishes you, then gives you one charged moment of approval that feels like oxygen.

> *Trauma bonding keeps the old regime emotionally alive inside you and keeps you craving the relief that intermittent reinforcement taught your nervous system.*

Ongoing Retaliation and Induced Fear

Controllers do not often need to state the threat directly. The implication is enough.

You know what may happen if you push back. You know what access may close, what story may circulate, what contact may be cut, what loyalty test may appear, what punishment may come dressed as neutrality, professionalism, discipline, or family disappointment.

> *Fear does not require certainty. It only requires enough data that your body starts making conservative choices around someone else's power.*

Smear Campaigns

You may have been told to protect the Controller's privacy while your own reputation remained fair game.

That asymmetry matters.

The smear may be explicit, though it is often cumulative. A portrait of you as unstable, disloyal, difficult, ungrateful, unwell, irrational, not a team player, not a good family member, not committed enough, too ambitious, too emotional, too much. The story begins circulating before you realize you need to defend yourself, if it is even safe to try.

> *Smear campaigns widen the Dead Zone by recruiting other people into the distortion.*

Gag Orders

> *Coercive systems often try to manage who you can speak to, what you can say, and which parts of reality are allowed to become shared reality. In contrast, your privacy is violated at the Controller's discretion.*

This can happen formally through non-disclosure agreements, legal threats, or institutional processes. It can happen informally through shame, loyalty demands, family secrecy, coaching culture, professional norms, or the repeated message that certain truths would be destructive, disloyal, immature, or career-ending to reveal.

A gag order does not have to use those words to do its work.

Quiet Humiliation

Some humiliations are loud. Many are not.

A joke at your expense. A correction in front of other people. Your vulnerability was later used against you. Your love made embarrassing. Your body was evaluated. Your work is underacknowledged. Your dignity is treated as optional. Your contribution was casually bypassed. A family meal, a gathering, a car ride, a holiday, a mediation, a dinner with investors, any scene in which the atmosphere tells you clearly that your comfort matters less.

> *Quiet humiliation is powerful because it can be so easily denied by the person who benefits from it.*

Sexual Coercion

> *Sexual coercion is any pattern in which your consent, pace, timing, preference, or bodily autonomy is treated as secondary to the Controller's entitlement or pleasure.*

That may include pressure, monitoring, comparison, withholding, tallying, keeping an intercourse frequency tracker, sleep disruption, touching that overrides your cues, expectation disguised as intimacy, or the reduction of your erotic life into a metric of compliance or value. In romance, this may be explicit. In coaching or workplace settings, the sexualization may come through atmosphere, implication, boundary pressure, or exploitation of dependency and rank.

Your body is not a performance review.

Financial Dependency

Money is one of coercive control's favorite solvents because it dissolves options.

Your earning power may be discouraged, or made secondary. Your spending may be policed. Your transparency may be required while theirs remains optional.

> *You may be encouraged to fuse finances in ways that reduce your leverage and increase theirs.*

You may be talked out of work, independence, legal protections, or practical exits. You may be told the arrangement is for your future, your family, your stability, your chance, your success, your team, or your bond.

Then, once dependence is in place, that dependence is used against you.

Legal and Institutional Betrayal

Coercive control often gains force by manipulating the systems people are supposed to trust.

Courts. Mediators. Lawyers. School systems. Human resources. Teams. Boards. Churches. Extended family. Professional networks. These systems can become extensions of the original domination when they absorb the Controller's distortions, underestimate the coercion, or prioritize preserving order over understanding power.

> *Institutional betrayal lands so hard because it attacks the belief that the rules might still protect you.*

Installed Blame

Installed blame is the way coercive control keeps your attention pointed inward and backward, rather than outward and forward.

You keep replaying the moments where you tolerated, explained away, delayed, accommodated, forgave, stayed, returned, performed, overworked, appeased, shrank, or hoped.

> *Installed blame is useful to coercive systems because it diverts attention from the structure and turns you into the custodian of your own indictment.*

It is one more Dirty Bomb. It keeps the old regime living rent-free in your mind.

The Discard

Without transparency, the Controller engineers your abrupt ouster from the relationship system at your expense and without regard for your humanity or prior promises.

Because the Discard so often multiplies every other injury, it deserves more than one line in a list.

The Discard: A Coward's Retreat

The Discard is not an ordinary ending.

It is a maladaptive, manipulative, rank-restoring way to end a bond while attempting to keep an unfair advantage.

The Discard lacks transparency. It tries to arrange the end in a way that protects the Controller's preferred story, punishes your separateness, and leaves you contaminated with enough confusion, shame, and longing that part of your attention remains tied to the old system. The Controller may want a new Mark, a better resource, a cleaner image, more legal advantage, less friction, or simpler access to the next chapter of their life. The Discard helps them move while you are still disoriented.

This happens in romance most obviously. A lockout. A sudden ending after repeated denials that anything had changed. An abrupt downgrade. An accusation that flips the story. But the same structure can appear elsewhere. A boss sidelines, expels, or publicly recasts the employee once the employee becomes inconvenient. A mentor goes cold and revisionist after taking years of loyalty and labor. A family system ejects or scapegoats the member who stopped carrying its burdens. A coach freezes out the athlete whose body, conscience, or questions have become inconvenient to the program.

The ending tries to make your displacement look like a verdict on your worth.

That is the lie.

> *The Discard is a coward's retreat from accountability. It is the system revealing itself. It is an extension of the abuse of coercive control.*

You are not only left. You are left in a way that tries to reshape the narrative around the Controller's convenience. The future you were taught to believe in is withdrawn or hollowed out. What was framed as devotion.

Once the structure is named, the Discard starts reading differently. What felt like a final judgment begins to look like another coercive move within a larger regime. The same person or system that revised reality during the relationship now revises the ending.

> *If the bond had been organized around equal humanity, the ending would not need this much manipulation.*

Why the Discard Burns

The Discard intensifies shame, trauma bonding, identity erosion, longing, and self-attack. It tempts you to believe that being left, downgraded, or replaced determines your value. It keeps the mind searching for the one better move that would have preserved the bond. It invites you to spend your energy proving your worth, defending your reality, or extracting moral coherence from a system that has already shown its contempt for equal terms.

That is why the Discard belongs with Dirty Bombs.

It is an impact multiplier.

When You See Remnants of the Controller: A Post-Contact Reset

Even after you have left the coercive system, the system may still know how to reach your body fast.

A sighting. A legal encounter. A voice. A message. A forced shared space. A photograph. A public event. A professional setting. A family gathering. A tournament. An office.

After contact, you may find yourself thinking about the betrayal more than you did days earlier. This does not necessarily mean you are moving backward. It often means the old field was reactivated.

Your body reads exposure before your mind has language for it. Then the mind gets recruited into cleanup. It starts scanning again for danger, moral explanation, and the one thing you still have not solved. Betrayal, humiliation, fear, grief, disgust, anger, and fatigue all rise at once.

This is a normal post-contact effect.

> *Your task after contact is not to decode the Controller more accurately. Your task is to reduce the afterlife of the encounter. Name it plainly:* **Dead Zone hangover.**

Treat the increase in thinking as residue, not revelation. Refuse unpaid interpretive labor. Return to food, water, sleep, routine, and low-stakes tasks. Help your body stand down.

The goal is to regain custody of yourself.

In summary, this chapter is here to help you stop underestimating the scale of what happened because each tactic, by itself, was so easy to dismiss.

That is how coercive control survives recognition. It fragments itself. It presents one incident at a time and lets the target absorb the cumulative cost in private.

You do not need to keep granting it that advantage.

Once the tactics are named, the shame starts losing some of its power. The hidden costs begin to form a pattern. That matters because once you recognize the pattern you can interrupt it.

I created the CoerciveControlRecovery.com website to accompany this book to assist you as you head toward a better horizon. One dynamic tool is ready for you, and I'm excited to describe that next.

One of the clearest ways to regain the helm is to assess the impact coercive control had on your life with honesty and structure. That is why I created **Check Your Bearings™: A Recovery Tracker for Life After Coercive Control** as a companion to this book. Your first tracker establishes a fuller map across **Before, During, End, and Now** so you can see both the damage and the progress already made. After that, you can return every 12 weeks using **Now** only, keeping your own private record and tracking your recovery toward a better horizon.

Check Your Bearings™: A Recovery Tracker for Life After Coercive Control

By this point, you may already know the pattern. What many survivors still do not know is the scale of it.

Coercive control trains you to minimize. It breaks things apart, hides the cumulative cost, and leaves you arguing over individual moments while the larger damage keeps spreading. That is one reason people often emerge from coercive systems with a strange split in their minds. They know something serious happened. They also keep discounting the evidence of their own erosion.

I developed **Check Your Bearings™** to interrupt that erasure.

When you complete the tracker, whether on paper or on the website, your first assessment provides a broader map across **Before, During, End, and Now**. That first pass is meant to help you see the full arc of impact and recognize what recovery may already be underway. Many survivors are clearer, stronger, or further rebuilt than they feel on the inside. A fuller map helps make that visible.

After your first assessment, you can return to **Check Your Bearings**™ every 12 weeks and rate **Now** only. This allows you to track recovery over time without having to re-enter the full history. For privacy, keep your earlier scores in your own records so you can compare them over time and watch your course realign.

This tracker is not a test of whether you were strong enough, smart enough, or badly damaged enough. It shows where the storm made landfall. Some readers will see only a few domains flare. Others will light up across the whole chart. Neither outcome is proof of weakness. It is proof of exposure.

Many ways of measuring coercive control focus primarily on what the Controller did. That is helpful. **Check Your Bearings**™ builds on this and asks what the regime did to you. What happened to your self-trust, your body, your work, your time, your money, your voice, your relationships, your freedom, your sense of future, and your sense that your life was still fully yours?

Check Your Bearings™ is built to help you see the spread.

It tracks the impact across the areas of life that coercive control most often colonizes. It also helps separate three things that often get blurred together:
- **impact**
- **exposure or tactics**
- **acute safety markers**

Those are related. They are not identical.

A person may have a significant impact even if outsiders consider the visible incidents small. Another may have severe exposure and still minimize the aftermath. Another may be in immediate danger. The point of **Check Your Bearings™** is not to flatten those distinctions. It is to make them easier to see.

Recovery does not begin with, "Now I understand it, so I should be over it." Recovery begins when the damaged territory is clearly identified enough that repair becomes practical. We do not heal by demanding instant transformation from a nervous system and a life that was trained under pressure. We heal by locating what was colonized, what is still carrying a burden, and what must now be restored to your own custody.

Check Your Bearings™ is a way to begin that mapping. Use it gently. The goal is to reveal where it spread, what has already begun to heal, and where your recovery now requires the most care.

From there, you can begin building not only insight, but a plan.

Chapter Four

What Was Stolen

By the time coercive control is finally clear enough to name, many survivors are already asking versions of the same question.

Why am I still so affected?
Why can't I move on?
Why do I feel so changed if the harm looked so deniable from the outside?
Why do I feel like so much was lost?

Those questions make sense. They are also too narrow for the sea you crossed.

A better question is this:

What was stolen?

That question changes the frame.

It stops treating your suffering like a mysterious overreaction and starts reading it as evidence of theft.

> *Coercive control is not only painful. It takes. It takes in ways that can look ordinary while the taking is underway. It takes through pressure, through hope, through correction, through silence, through role assignment, through strategic confusion, through future faking, through love fraud, through the manufacture of kindness, through everyday rearrangement, through the endless small conversions by which your life becomes easier to use and harder to inhabit.*

What gets stolen is rarely one thing.

In romance, the theft may move through attachment, time, privacy, hope, and home. In a narcissistic family system, it may move through belonging, role capture, guilt, duty, and emotional labor. At work, it may move through authorship, promotion, credit, reputation, and your relationship to your own ambition. In mentorship, it may move through self-trust, dependence, future orientation, and the right to develop outside the mentor's shadow. In sport, it may move through bodily sovereignty, confidence, identity, and the future you thought your discipline was building.

The surface differs. The theft does not.

Time

Time is one of the first things coercive control steals because time is what all the other thefts ride in on.

Hours spent explaining. Waiting. Bracing. Recovering. Replaying. Rehearsing. Managing mood. Preparing for conversations that never make progress. Repairing confusion that should never have existed. Becoming smaller so the weather might stay calm a little longer.

A partner can take time this way. So can a family system that keeps you permanently managing emotional weather. So can the boss whose ambiguity eats your evenings, the mentor whose crises become your bandwidth, the coach whose demands colonize your days long after practice ends.

> *Time theft is particularly cruel because it is so hard to bill. When people look back, they often see years where almost nothing was formally "taken," yet huge parts of life never really belonged to them while they were living it.*

Attention

Attention becomes occupied territory.

You stop spending your best mental energy on your own work, rest, friendships, creativity, plans, and future. Your attention gets pulled into the system. Into the household atmosphere. Into the boss's next mood or campaign. Into the family drama. Into the mentor's expectations. Into the coach's response.

That occupation creates a tax.

Ordinary life starts costing more concentration than it used to because so much of your attention is no longer free. It is tied up in management, interpretation, and self-interruption.

Privacy

Privacy gets stolen directly and indirectly.

Sometimes the theft is obvious: questions, monitoring, access to devices and cameras, demands for transparency, financial scrutiny, body commentary, and control over who you see and what you say.

> *Sometimes the theft is atmospheric. You become so used to scrutiny that you surrender privacy in advance.*

You narrate your whereabouts before anyone asks. You rehearse explanations before a question is posed. You hide friendships, ambitions, purchases, plans, preferences, or inner life because privacy no longer feels like an unquestioned right. Then you are accused of secrecy and dishonesty.

That is one of coercive control's quieter victories. You start cooperating with the loss of your own perimeter just to reduce friction.

Confidence

Not performance confidence. Not bravado.

The quieter confidence.

The kind that lets you trust your memory, hold a boundary, choose a course, keep your sense of proportion without needing outside ratification for what you already know.

Coercive control erodes that confidence by making clarity expensive. You begin second-guessing what you saw, what you meant, what you concluded, what you wanted, what you have the right to insist on. That erosion can happen in a marriage, a family, a job, a mentorship, or under a coach.

> *Anywhere rank becomes more central than truth,*
> *confidence starts taking hits.*

Ease

Ease is often stolen before you realize it.

Ease in your own home. Ease in your own body. Ease in your own office, your own team, your own routines, your own friendships. Ease in laughter, rest, play, pacing, speech, movement, and ordinary wanting.

You begin moving through life with a little more tension, a little less spontaneity. You become more defensive in places that used to feel livable.

> *When ease goes missing, people often blame themselves*
> *for becoming rigid, tired, or joyless. Often, they were living*
> *in a system that had made ease too expensive to maintain.*

Reputation

Reputation theft matters because it changes what the world will let you do next. Coercive control often works by feeding other people altered versions of you. Subtly unstable. Less credible. More selfish. More emotional. More demanding. Less talented than your work suggests. Less steady than your actual behavior would support.

Sometimes the campaign is open. Often it is cumulative poison. It is isolating and dangerous.

This happens in romance through friend groups, family networks, and legal settings. In families, it happens through roles and inherited narratives. At work, it can determine advancement, trust, authorship, and who gets heard. In mentorship and coaching, it can change how your future is narrated before you even know a story is circulating.

Reputation theft restricts possibility. It reshapes the waters around you before you know you are swimming in altered conditions.

Desire

Desire does not always disappear. It often becomes too expensive to inhabit.

You still want things in theory. Work you care about. Rest. Sex on your own terms. Travel. Creativity. Love without occupation. Privacy. Self-respect. But the route to wanting becomes crowded. Desire begins to feel indulgent, dangerous, badly timed, unrealistic, disloyal, or somehow beyond your proper rank.

This is one of the more devastating thefts. The future starts to look less like something you inhabit and more like something you manage with permission.

Continuity

Coercive control disrupts the continuity of the self.

The you who used to move with more coherence starts feeling far away. Your old standards, confidence, rhythms, work habits, friendships, humor, style of thought, appetite for life, and sense of your own future become harder to access. You are still functioning. You may even be functioning impressively. Yet the thread connecting your current self to your wider life begins to fray.

This is one reason people so often say, "I don't feel like myself," after coercive control. Not because the self has vanished. Because continuity was repeatedly interrupted by a system that demanded adaptation.

What This Means

This is the point at which many survivors begin to realize the problem was never only the fight, the betrayal, the difficult person, the humiliation, the bad meeting, the legal disaster, the role, or the breakup. The problem was that an entire section of life became organized around surviving the system.

That kind of theft can leave you looking functional on the outside while quietly being looted on the inside. It can leave you questioning whether you are even entitled to grieve because much of what was stolen was intangible. You still have the résumé, but it doesn't convey the same confidence. The house, but not the same ease. The family, but not the same authority. The career, but not the same appetite. The body, but not the same sense that it belongs to you, without negotiation. The memories, but not the same continuity of self.

> *Your life became organized around preserving the Controller's primacy.*

> *That is theft.*

And it is one reason survivors so often get stuck in the aftermath. The theft was real, but the surrounding culture still wants more obvious evidence before it agrees that something valuable was taken. More bruising. More spectacle. More official language. Coercive control thrives in that gap.

Dispossession can still look like relationship, family duty, leadership, ambition, loyalty, discipline, mentorship, or love when viewed from a distance.

You no longer need to adopt that distance. One way to gain a more empowering perspective is to continue educating yourself on how to move into your next chapter. This book and the companion website CoerciveControlRecovery.com are available to you for that very reason.

Personhood Was Stolen

What was stolen was not only time, money, privacy, stability, or recognition.

What was stolen was your personhood, and it was not taken all at once. It was taken through time claimed from your life, through bandwidth occupied, through self-trust worn down, and through the steady insult of being treated less as a full person than as a function inside someone else's system.

That is why robust recovery is not simply "getting over" a coercive person, an exploitative boss, a narcissistic family system, an abusive coach, or a predatory mentor.

Recovery reclaims occupied territory.

It restores the conditions under which your life can become inhabitable again, as your own.

Dispossession

Dispossession happens when your life still appears to belong to you, while less of it remains under your control.

You may still have your name on the door, the account, the lease, the degree, the résumé, the team roster, the family photo, the office, the role. From the outside, enough of the structure remains intact that proving the loss can be hard. From the inside, something has shifted.

That is why dispossession can be hard to name. Many people expect theft to announce itself with something visible and final. A house taken. An account is empty. A firing. A public expulsion. Those count. Coercive control can also dispossess more quietly.

One way to understand dispossession is through ordinary norms. You move through life assuming some basic rules still hold. You trust the crosswalk when the "Walk" signal is lit. Then the truck comes through anyway, and you are left injured while being blamed for trusting the signal. The first injury is the strike. The second is the attack on your confidence that the rules were ever meant to protect you. Coercive control works that second injury hard. It tries to dispossess you of confidence in your own judgment and your right to expect fair treatment.

That is why the loss cuts so deep. The wound is not limited to resources. The wound reaches into your belief that your life was ever allowed to be safely yours.

Dispossession often spreads through repetition. Your time gets pre-claimed. Work becomes harder to protect. Travel is rerouted. Your money buys more scrutiny than freedom. Your inner life begins to disintegrate because so much energy is diverted to self-interruption. The institutions and social expectations you trusted become easier for the coercive system to bend in its favor.

The pain grows sharper because enough outward normalcy can remain in place that you doubt your own right to call it theft. You may still be functioning. You may still be in the home, the marriage, the family, the company, the mentorship, the team. Yet what should belong to you now comes with friction, penalty, override, or quiet resistance. You remain present while losing custody over the terms under which your life is lived.

That is dispossession.

The pattern can move through many routes. Through housing. Through finances. Through family role. Through sexuality. Through work. Through cognition. Through moral pressure. Through the slow weakening of your authority over your own days.

> *You may still have formal membership in the relationship or the institution while losing real authority inside it. That is one reason coercive control can feel faintly caste-like. Your presence remains useful. Your standing does not remain equal.*

Many survivors first answer dispossession with self-criticism. I got weak. I lost my edge. I became dependent. I got disorganized. I made bad choices. Those conclusions arrive downstream from a structural shift. A controlling system made it harder to maintain ordinary ownership of your own life.

One woman left mediation still trying to understand how so much had been taken from her so quickly. What tormented her was not only the outcome on paper. She had been maneuvered out of retirement security, disability protection, and the home she thought would anchor her future. Afterward, her mind kept running the tape. Every concession. Every exchange. Every turn where she might have said something different. What unsettled her most was how easily her lawyer and the mediator absorbed the predator's distortions of her and softened his threatening behavior. She blamed herself for following weak legal advice and kept searching for a better move, the moment when she might have stopped the loss.

That is one face of dispossession. The mind reaches for a clearer explanation because the alternative feels harder to bear. She wanted to believe the loss exposed a defect in her judgment rather than the fact that she entered a contaminated field after a long period of destabilization, pressure, fear, and insomnia. By the time she reached the table, her self-trust had already been worn down. The ground beneath her had already been shaped against her.

> *What looked like a bad negotiation was the late expression of a larger coercive regime. The abuse had simply changed settings.*

That kind of harm leaves more than financial damage. It leaves moral injury. It leaves cultural betrayal. It leaves the shock of learning that the rules you trusted can be violated and then turned against you.

Dispossession can happen through norms bent against you, through money controlled and spending policed, through domestic life organized around someone else's primacy, through relationships where your availability is expected while theirs remains optional, through cognition weakened by constant override, and through moral life distorted until your own values become difficult to fully live. None of these losses needs a dramatic seizure to count.

> *Constant low-grade compromise can still separate you from your own life with efficiency.*

When you reduce yourself to preserve access to what should already be yours, you are adapting to dispossession.

Recovery begins when that adaptation is named clearly. Once you can see where your authority was downgraded, the pattern stops looking like scattered strain and starts reading as what it was. A system that made your life harder to inhabit while leaving you to explain the damage as if it began in you.

The next theft grows inside that same terrain.

Unpaid emotional labor.

Emotional Labor

Emotional labor inside coercive control runs deeper than visible tasks.

You may still think of labor in older terms. Meals cooked. Bills paid. Crises handled. Schedules managed. Laundry folded. Travel arranged. Those forms of work count. Emotional labor adds another layer. It is the ongoing effort of responding to a human weather pattern that claims more space than it should. You become the stabilizer, the interpreter, the shock absorber, the one who notices tone, tracks tension, predicts fallout, and adjusts the atmosphere before the next drop in pressure clouds the moment or becomes a storm.

That work often stays invisible because the system benefits from hiding it.

In a controlling relationship, your emotional steadiness becomes part of the other person's regulation. In a narcissistic family system, your maturity becomes a staffing plan. In a workplace, your diplomacy gets used to cushion the boss's volatility or ego. In mentorship, your deference and admiration become part of the mentor's private supply. In coaching, your discipline and self-suppression become part of the culture that keeps the program looking strong from the outside.

The labor can look noble while it is happening. Supportive. Flexible. Loyal. Professional. Team-minded. Some of those qualities may truly belong to you. The issue is what the coercive system did with them and what it costs you to keep providing them under unequal conditions.

> *One of the crueler features of emotional labor is that the better you carry it, the easier your continued carrying becomes for everyone else to ignore.*

You monitor tone, timing, pacing, mood, and risk. You steady the room. You absorb the spillover. You rehearse the conversation in advance. You explain things carefully enough to reduce the risk of retaliation. You do extra work, so someone else's unpredictability does less damage. From the outside, you can look capable. From the inside, you may feel spent.

> *And, after all that work, if something goes wrong, you are even more likely to be blamed because the overworking has put you in situations that make it easy to scapegoat you.*

That cost builds.

Exploited emotional labor leaves residue in the body and mind. Panic. Irritability. Sleep disruption. Overthinking. The feeling that you were somehow always working, even in moments that were supposed to be restful. You were working. The system was just careful not to call it that.

Emotional labor also includes the work of self-reduction. You decide what not to say, what not to ask for, what not to want, whether the issue is worth the cost of naming it, and whether the relationship or role can survive your honesty. You whittle yourself down in real time. That quiet editing is labor too.

In many coercive systems, you also become the archivist. You keep track of what was promised, what shifted, what got denied, what changed, what was said in one room and contradicted in another. Even if nothing is written down, your body and mind begin storing pattern data. That effort can feed rumination later because the system taught you that coherence would not be protected unless you tried to protect it yourself.

Emotional labor distorts intimacy and belonging. Instead of feeling met, you feel tasked. Instead of feeling known, you feel used for your capacities. In romance, the bond can begin feeling less like mutuality and more like management. In family life, closeness can become a permanent burden. At work, "leadership" can become

high ground in the same movement. Public handling shapes the social story of you before you have spoken. *Legal abuse* recruits institutions into the distortion.

These tactics show up in every coercive setting. In romance, a partner may rewrite promises, intentions, or the meaning of clear behavior. In family systems, one person's authority over the story can become so entrenched that one's pain gets filtered through disloyalty before it is heard. At work, the boss's version carries more weight than the subordinate's lived experience. In mentorship, the guide's interpretation of your motives can begin to replace your own. In coaching, the athlete's body and limits may be overwritten by the program's story about discipline or commitment.

Reality theft damages more than cognition. It weakens boundaries, slows decisions, harms social support, and deepens fatigue. When your reading of reality keeps getting challenged, acting on your own judgment starts to feel strangely dangerous. You hesitate. You seek extra confirmation. You over-explain. You keep trying to produce the final evidence packet that will make the story undeniable.

Some of that effort may be legally or professionally necessary. Some of it belongs to the trauma loop that reality theft installed.

The rumination keeps your attention arrested. It keeps you oriented backward. It keeps the original asymmetry alive, with the Controller still holding too much power to ratify or refuse your experience. That is why recovery eventually must move beyond convincing and toward anchoring.

Anchoring begins with a cleaner relationship to truth. What is true? What evidence do I need for practical reasons? What am I still trying to prove to a system that benefited from my doubt? Determine what attention belongs to the past because it serves protection, legal necessity, or coherence. Ask what attention now belongs to my future.

There is a broader social layer here, too.

> *Ranked systems grant greater interpretive latitude to those with more status, money, charisma, institutional backing, or centrality.*

Their complexity gets honored. The subordinate party gets suspicion, tone-policing, motive analysis, and the burden of proof. That is one reason reality theft can feel collective even when it began in private. The culture is often ready to assume that the person with more rank also has more reality.

One talented employee learned that lesson under a corporate boss who praised him as a rising leader and gave him visible responsibility. The arrangement looked like sponsorship. In practice, the boss was harvesting ideas, labor, and credibility while keeping real authority and credit for himself. When the employee later tried to claim authorship of his own work and correct a distorted account of what had happened, rank closed over the truth. The boss's version carried more weight. The employee's account was treated as self-interested. What began as false empowerment hardened into dispossession through hierarchy.

That is how reality theft works. It not only confuses the target. It reshapes the social field around the target.

Recovery means returning custody. You stop waiting for the old system to validate your truth. You keep a clear record where needed. You preserve what happened outside the distortion field. You practice one or two sentences you no longer negotiate. You stop treating your own humanity as a matter for debate.

When reality returns to your custody, the chart returns to your hands. You lose less life to rehashing, re-proving, and re-entering old courtrooms in your head. Clarity with compassion restores movement.

That is the turn. Clarity is reinforced by community outside of the Dead Zone. Find others who've made the same journey at the book's companion website CoerciveControlRecovery.com.

Once your own reading is no longer hostage to the old regime, you can begin living by it.

Chapter Five
The Dead Zone

The Dead Zone is the environment created when coercive control has sunk so deeply into your life that it no longer needs constant, visible force to shape it. By then, the system has already entered your body, your self-talk, your routines, your expectations, and your sense of what is possible. The pressure may not look dramatic from the outside. The occupation continues all the same.

That is what makes the Dead Zone so confusing. People often expect domination to look loud. Sometimes it does. Just as often, the system has moved past spectacle. The hierarchy is installed. The penalties are understood. The atmosphere does the work. You begin adapting before anyone must correct you. You begin shrinking before anyone demands it. I can't tell you how many of my coaching clients have described sitting in a room where they are being told by others that they are "lucky" to have the Controller in their life because they only see the carefully manicured outer image maintained by the coercive system.

The Dead Zone is where diminished life starts to feel ordinary.

You may remember stretches when nothing visibly catastrophic was happening, yet your life still felt oxygen-starved. Tasks took more effort than they should have. Rest did not restore much. Initiative stalled. Ordinary choices carried hidden freight. You were in poisoned water, weakened drip by drip.

That distinction matters. Many survivors lose years trying to understand why they felt so bad in periods that looked, from the outside, relatively calm. The answer is that the system already ruled the climate. Once that happens, visible conflict is no longer required for your life to keep narrowing. The pressure has moved inward. You live under its weather from the inside.

In a controlling relationship, this can look like a house in which the Controller's agenda quietly governs everyone else's range of motion. In a narcissistic family system, the Dead Zone may look like a shared atmosphere in which one person's fragility outranks everyone else's reality. At work, it may be the office where the boss's self-story shapes what can be said, challenged, or protected. In sport, it may be the team culture that increasingly treats your body, doubt, and limits as inconveniences to the program.

The setting changes. The injury has the same feel. More of you must retreat underground.

That is one reason the Dead Zone can persist after the visible bond has loosened or ended. The breakup happened. The job changed. The family visit ended. The coach lost access. The litigation is pending or complete. Outsiders assume the main issue is over because the most obvious contact has reduced. But inside, the older hierarchy may still be active. The penalties may still shape your thoughts.

This is where survivors often turn against themselves. They think they have become passive, weak, old, lazy, overreactive, indecisive, dramatic, too sensitive, or somehow constitutionally less alive than they once were. The Dead Zone feeds on that mistake. It wants you to read adaptation as identity. Once you do that, you are less of a threat to the coercive system.

A more accurate reading is available. You did not become passive, weak, or old. You became cautious in a climate where movement had consequences. You did not become lazy. You became depleted in a system that kept taxing your body and mind. You did not become indecisive. You were living in a place where decisions carried hidden costs.

You did not become smaller by nature. You were being slowly downgraded inside an atmosphere built to favor the Controller's primacy.

That is the truth the Dead Zone tries hardest to keep from you.

The body often reveals it first. Heaviness. Fog. Dread. The feeling of watching your own life from slightly outside it. The sense that some part of you has gone underground. These are responses to a system in which too much of ordinary life had to be lived against correction, uncertainty, and manipulation.

The Dead Zone also has a social layer. It rarely belongs solely to the Controller. It is reinforced by the little court that gathers around rank. Admirers. Dependents. Enablers. Beneficiaries. In-laws. Misogynistic or patriarchal societal norms. People who gain comfort, access, approval, or relief from staying aligned with the dominant weather. This can happen in families, companies, teams, churches, communities, friend groups, and social circles built around the Controller. The presence of that court makes the Dead Zone feel larger than the Controller, because in a sense it is. The atmosphere has been socially ratified.

That is one reason coercive control can feel strangely caste-like. The Controller remains closer to the center of what counts. Others organize around that center. You, the Mark, adapt, then get judged by the marks that adaptation leaves behind.

Once the Dead Zone is understood, many old confusions begin to clear. You stop asking why you could understand the pattern and still feel drained by it. You stop assuming that because you can describe the regime, you must already be fully out of it. Vocabulary helps. Vocabulary does not, by itself, drain poisoned water.

That is why recovery asks for more than insight. It asks for a change in climate. Different access. Different voices in your head. Different expectations of what love, work, family, belonging, guidance, and success are allowed to cost. The Dead Zone is where domination starts feeling practical. Recovery begins when that practicality is seen as a symptom of coercive control. Resources such as this book and the companion website, CoerciveControlRecovery.com, help you leave the Dead Zone behind.

You were trying to thrive in an atmosphere that had already downgraded you. No wonder it felt hard to live there.

Chapter Six
The Piracy of Personhood

Coercive control does more than injure you. It changes the terms under which your humanity is held.

> *That is why the aftermath can feel so strange. You are not only grieving events, losses, or a person. You are trying to recover from having been treated less as a full human being and more as a source of use.*

A function. A role. A convenience. A body. A servant to someone else's self-story. A person-shaped resource.

That is the piracy of personhood.

Some people hear the word dehumanization and imagine something glaring, theatrical, obviously cruel. Coercive control often works more quietly than that. Dehumanization can arrive in polite language, spiritual language, leadership language, and praise. It may look almost tender at first. The shift happens when your humanity stops acting as a limit in the Controller's mind. Once that limit is gone, more abuse becomes possible. Extraction becomes easier. Punishment becomes easier. Distortion becomes easier. Your hurt becomes easier to dismiss. Your separateness becomes easier to resent.

That shift is one of the ugliest parts of coercive control because it can coexist with periods of apparent warmth. A partner may still profess love. A family may still insist you belong. A boss may still call you valuable. A mentor may still claim to be invested in your future. A coach may still say they believe in you. None of that guarantees reverence for your personhood.

> *A person can want what you provide while holding your humanity in lower regard than their own comfort, ambition, image, or need for control.*

That is the downgrade.

Your trust stops being sacred and becomes access. Your labor stops being honored and begins to be taken for granted.

Over time, this repeated handling leaves marks. Some of them are emotional. Some are bodily. Some are moral. Some live in the way you move through a room, how quickly you apologize, how much of yourself you edit before speaking, how little right you feel to take up your own life without justification.

One of the most efficient ways the piracy of personhood takes hold is through **carried shame**.

Carried Shame

Carried shame happens when someone else behaves without conscience, and you end up holding the moral burden as if it were yours.

Something degrading happens. Something beneath the standards you once believed would hold. Then, instead of your mind landing cleanly on the fact that you were manipulated, lied to, overruled, diminished, exploited, or exposed to a system organized around your reduction, the blade turns inward. You should have known. You should have left sooner. You were pathetic. You betrayed yourself.

That is carried shame.

The shame feels real. Its assignment is false.

> *The Controller extracts without naming the cost, leaving you feeling morally contaminated.*

The family system humiliates you, and you end up feeling disloyal for noticing. The boss steals credit, and you end up feeling needy for wanting recognition. The mentor manipulates your dependence, and you end up feeling foolish for trusting. The coach punishes your limits, and you end up feeling soft or defective for having a body.

Carried shame is useful to coercive systems because it traps you in self-interrogation rather than in appraising the structure. It silences. It isolates. It turns a public injury into a private accusation. It keeps your attention pointed inward and backward.

That is why shame lingers so long after contact ends. It has been installed as part of the aftermath.

Shame grows especially well in people who were already used to carrying too much. People who were praised for maturity. People who learned early to preserve the peace. People who pride themselves on competence, conscience, and emotional intelligence. Shame takes those good qualities and turns them into weapons against the self.

That move deserves a clear name. The presence of shame does not prove guilt. It often proves exposure to somebody else's shamelessness.

Recovery begins when you start relocating the burden. What happened that I am still assigning to myself? What standard did I supposedly violate? What standard did they violate while I was busy carrying the bill?

Those questions alone can change the weather.

Dehumanization

Dehumanization is what makes coercive control possible.

Before someone can repeatedly extract from you, reorganize your life, punish your separateness, distort your reality, or use your strengths without naming the cost, your humanity must lose status in their internal order. They may still admire you. They may still need you. They may still desire you. They may still praise you. None of that prevents dehumanization. Sometimes it helps disguise it.

You are no longer being met first as a full person whose subjectivity carries weight. You are being met as yield. Yield for romance, family stability, business growth, the mentor's identity, the team, the program, for someone else's comfort, vanity, regulation, or advantage.

That is why the pain can feel deeper than heartbreak or disappointment.

> *You come to understand that your full personhood was never allowed equal standing in the room. You were permitted inside the arrangement so long as your presence supported extraction.*

That recognition can produce a very specific grief. You not only lose the relationship, the role, the team, the family fantasy, the mentor, the future, and the job. You lose the illusion that your humanity was being held under equal terms and that your trust was treated with the dignity it deserved.

Many survivors resist this conclusion for a long time because it hurts too much. They would rather preserve some part of the Controller's seduction story. He loved me in his way. She cared, just badly. They were flawed, not dehumanizing. Sometimes those thoughts hold fragments of truth. They also often serve as a form of pain management. They soften the blow of realizing that usefulness may have mattered more in the system than your personhood did.

That is why dehumanization must be named. The issue is not whether there were also moments of warmth, admiration, dependence, pride, or attachment. The issue is whether your humanity continued to operate as a limit on what the system felt entitled to do with you, or whether it was ignored.

If that limit kept disappearing, then the piracy of personhood was already underway.

How Dehumanization Naturalizes Itself

One of coercive control's ugliest tricks is that it causes the injury, then points to the injury as proof that the ranking was justified.

You shrink because shrinking reduces conflict. Then the shrinkage gets treated as evidence that you were smaller all along. You lose confidence after enduring repeated penalties for separateness, and that loss of confidence gets treated as proof that you were dependent or inadequate. You become exhausted from defending your reality, and that exhaustion gets read as instability, weakness, or poor character. You begin doubting yourself because you have lived too long in distortion, and that doubt gets offered back to you as evidence that your judgment was always flawed.

That is how domination naturalizes itself.

> *The system creates the wound, then uses it as evidence that your lower standing was appropriate.*

This can happen in any coercive setting. The partner who first exploits dependence later despises you for needing reassurance or stability. The family that punishes differentiation later treats your hesitation as evidence that you were always too fragile or difficult. The boss who undercuts your standing later cites your diminished confidence as a reason not to advance you. The mentor who keeps you entangled later reads your uncertainty as proof that you still need their guidance. The coach who trains you to override your body later treats the injury, fear, or weariness as evidence that you lacked the right character from the start.

That inversion keeps people trapped for years.

Stowaways: Coercion in the Body

The body keeps score in ways the mind may still be trying to tidy up.

Coercive control reaches the body through breath, sleep, digestion, posture, libido, concentration, memory, hormones, immune function, and the tiny calculations by which a moment gets judged safe enough to inhabit. The body learns the territory. It learns which times of day bring pressure. Which messages tighten the chest? Which silences mean trouble? Which glances warn of correction or silent, damning judgment? Which kinds of praise feel dangerous? Which absences do not bring relief because the nervous system has not yet been persuaded that the storm has passed?

That learning can feel humiliating when you do not yet have the language for it. Why am I still reacting? Why am I so tired? Why does my heart race before my mind catches up? Why does this feel bigger than the visible moment?

Because the body was trained under coercion.

The body can carry contradiction too. Longing and fear at once. Relief and grief in the same breath. Desire and revulsion collide. Attachment and disgust braided into one response. That confusion does not mean you are irrational. It means the body learned a system in which comfort and threat were repeatedly delivered by the same source.

Sleep often becomes one of the clearest witnesses. Many survivors live with a kind of night watch after coercive control. The mind begins scanning, replaying, rehearsing, trying to get ahead of danger that has already happened. That makes sense. A system that relied on anticipation taught your body that vigilance might save you from some negative consequence. Later, the body must learn a different lesson. The danger passed. Rest no longer counts as betrayal of survival.

The body also carries old maps that predate the current Controller. Earlier family hierarchies. Previous training in appeasing, carrying, pleasing, over-functioning, peacemaking, and disappearing. Coercive control often finds those older pathways and uses them. That overlap can intensify shame. I should have seen it. I should have known.

> *A controlling system found a body already trained to survive difficult weather.*
>
> *That is not failure. That is pattern overlap.*

Recovery in the body begins with steadier evidence. Safer rhythms. Better sleep. Less interruption. More privacy. More pleasure without penalty. Movement for your own sake. Eating without scrutiny. Dressing without an audience. A home routine that does not organize itself around the Controller's standards. These are not cosmetic gains. They are anti-coercive acts. They teach the body that your life is returning to your own hands.

Pining for the Pirate

One of the cruelest aftereffects of coercive control is that you may still miss what hurt you.

You may miss the person, the role, the household, the family fantasy, the mentor, the team, the boss, the sense of purpose, the feeling of being chosen, the imagined future, the old charge of belonging. That longing can make smart people distrust themselves. They think that if the system were truly harmful, the pull would be gone by now.

Longing proves very little about the morality of the bond. It proves much more about how attachment, hope, relief, fear, intermittent reward, and identity became braided together.

Coercive control works through inconsistency. It gives and takes. Raises hope and then taxes it. Offers relief and ties that relief to control. Leaves you lonely and then offers rescue from the loneliness it helped produce. That rhythm creates an undertow. The body and mind can remain attached to the place where the wound kept reopening because the same place kept supplying moments of temporary relief.

That is why longing so often survives clarity.

You are not only withdrawing from harm. You are withdrawing from the structures into which you poured labor, devotion, time, and imagination. The relationship was supposed to become mutual. The family was supposed to become solid. The job was supposed to become recognized. The mentorship was supposed to become guidance. The team that was supposed to become home.

That is why people feel split against themselves. A part of them can see the system clearly. Another part still reaches toward the old harbor.

Longing becomes less dangerous when it gets more precise. What do you miss? The person, or the feeling of being chosen. The family, or the hope of finally being accepted. The job, or the charge of purpose and proximity to power. The mentor, or the fantasy that your future was being faithfully held. The team, or the intensity of belonging. The bond itself, or the moments of relief that interrupted the pain.

That precision matters. It helps separate the human need from the coercive structure that captured it.

> *You are allowed to miss what you once believed was being built. You are allowed to grieve the role, the fantasy, the future, the person you thought existed under the weather. Grief does not require reenlistment.*

Missing what hurt you does not make it home.

The Return of Personhood

The opposite of coercive control is not merely distance from the Controller. The opposite is the return of personhood. That return happens in ordinary actions. You stop relating to yourself as a function inside someone else's system. You stop treating usefulness as the price of worth, belonging, or love. You stop offering explanations to those who have used explanation as a route back into your life. You stop asking systems organized around your reduction to certify your humanity.

That change can be bittersweet. Some relationships, roles, and institutions become less attractive as your personhood returns. Some people get colder. Some become accusatory. Some lose interest. That loss carries information. They were more attached to what you provided than to who you were.

> *The return of personhood asks for standards. For privacy. For pleasure. For work that belongs to you. For limits. For rhythms that are not constantly broken by the Controller's demands. For the right to be imperfect, tired, erotic, private, complicated, grieving, joyful, firm, uncertain, and still fully worthy of respect.*

You were never only what you could provide. Dignity restores that border. How? You will now watch for who truly sees you as perfectly imperfect, who cares for you when you are seen as imperfect, and who wants to be present to you when you do absolutely nothing but share presence with them.

Personhood returns dignity to your custody.

Chapter Seven

Return to Your Own Chart

After coercive control, many people become wary of trust itself. That makes sense. If your trust is used as access, your hope as runway, your conscience as labor, and your reality as negotiable, caution can start to feel like the only intelligent response. Some people react by shutting down entirely. Some react by becoming hyperalert. Some try to build a life so tightly defended that nothing new can enter it at all. Some worry they will never trust again.

That response is understandable. It can also cost too much.

The goal of recovery is not permanent suspicion. The goal is the return of your instruments.

You do not need to become unreachable, loveless, or detached from ambition. You do need a more faithful way to read the weather.

> *Coercive control did not only wound you. It tried to disable your chart, contest your readings, and train you to mistake pressure for love, confusion for complexity, and diminishing terms for normal life.*

Recovery asks for the opposite. It asks for clearer readings, steadier standards, better use of time, and less willingness to hand over the helm to someone who sounds certain.

That is what this chapter is for.

Trust Yourself By Using RADAR

One practical way to reclaim your chart is to use what I call **RADAR**.

RADAR helps you detect coercive moves early enough that they do not harden into another regime. Controllers depend on speed, ambiguity, emotional capture, specialness, false urgency, and the interruption of your own appraisal. They want you to react to the weather rather than read it. They want you to answer bait rather than notice the objective beneath the bait. They want your focus on the moment while the structure goes unnamed.

RADAR helps reverse that.

The first move is to **read the move, not the excuse**.

Surface packaging can be very persuasive. A text may appear to raise a concern while serving as a compliance check. A question may sound innocent when seeking access. A gift may feel generous while quietly installing leverage. A criticism may present as feedback while reducing your standing. A delay may sound practical while keeping you off balance. A family appeal may sound loving while tightening the old role around your throat.

Reading the move means asking a harder question than what they say they mean. What function does this serve in the larger system? What gets widened for them and narrowed for me if I accept the surface story? If this were not about mutuality, what would it be about? Access. Control. Advantage. Image management. Position.

The next move is to **appraise the cost**.

Coercive systems thrive on minimization. They train you to say, "This is not that bad, this is only one moment, maybe I am overreacting, perhaps it is easier if I adapt." Appraisal interrupts that drift. It asks what the interaction does to your freedom. Do you leave the interaction feeling more solid or smaller? Clearer, or more fogged. More alive, or more occupied.

That question matters because many coercive moves are deniable on the surface while still costing dearly in the body and in the structure of daily life. The cost is the truth before the explanation catches up.

Then comes **detachment**.

Detachment means stepping outside the frame that coercive control is trying to build around you. The Controller wants urgency, emotional participation, self-justification, volunteered access, rushed answers, and proof of loyalty. Detachment breaks that sequence. You do not enter the courtroom simply because someone summoned you.

Detachment may look quiet from the outside. A delayed reply. A practical answer instead of an emotional defense. A walk before responding. A note to yourself rather than another round of confusing conversation. A call to someone outside the Dead Zone. A refusal to explain what has already been stated. A choice not to make your nervous system available for another performance of confusion.

From there, you **adjust**.

This is where many people lose traction. They understand the move, they feel the cost, they even mentally detach, yet nothing in the actual structure changes. Insight without adjustment can become one more way of privately surviving a system that remains practically untouched.

Instead, adjustment changes access, exposure, timing, expectation, and consequence. Fewer details shared. Less immediacy. Different channels. Longer gaps. Separate accounts. More privacy. A witness is present. A locked door. A revised routine. Fewer visits. No visits. Email only. Documented contact. A decision not to be alone with that person. A decision not to keep trying for mutuality when rank has already been installed. A decision not to let longing keep reopening the breach. No contact that includes no monitoring of the other's digital presence.

Adjustment can also be internal. You stop expecting fairness from a system organized around advantage. You stop expecting repair where there has been only denial. You stop expecting a coercive family system to bless your differentiation. You stop expecting an exploitative boss to become generous once the work gets good enough. You stop expecting a mentor who benefited from your dependence to celebrate your autonomy. You stop expecting the old structure to hand back your dignity voluntarily.

The final move is to **record**.

Coercive control depends on drift. Context gets altered. Calm returns just enough to tempt you into doubting what happened. A record interrupts that. A dated note. A screenshot. A line in a journal. A sentence about what happened in the room and what happened in your body. You are not recording to become obsessive. You are refusing the social amnesia that coercive control relies on.

When RADAR becomes a habit, something subtle begins to change. You become less interruptible by performance. Less available for bait. Less dependent on the other person's interpretation of what just occurred. You start responding to the pattern rather than to the packaging.

That shift matters. That shift is the helm returning.

Rejecting False Maps

One of the central injuries of coercive control is that it disturbs your confidence in your own map.

Reality was revised often enough that your own reading began losing standing, sometimes even to you. You may have known something was off, yet still felt unable to say it clearly. You may have sensed the breach in the hull long before you could prove it to yourself. That gap between knowing and certifying becomes one of the places coercive control lives longest.

Returning to your own chart means ending that arrangement.

You begin with a simple truth: what happened to you has shape, structure, and language. It was not random confusion.

It was not merely poor communication. It was not solved by being more loyal, more careful, more pleasing, more useful, more emotionally literate, more spiritually evolved, or more professional. A coercive system was acting on you. Once that becomes clear, you do not need the old regime's permission to name it.

That matters because many survivors remain partly trapped, trying to obtain final validation from the very people or institutions that benefited from their doubt. They want the apology that restores scale. The admission that restores proportion. The email, the meeting, the legal acknowledgment, the family correction, the institutional recognition, the mentor's confession, the coach's reckoning, the partner's honest sentence.

Those desires are deeply human. They can also keep the old asymmetry alive. If your reality remains contingent on the old system's ratification, then the old system still holds too much of it.

Returning to your own chart asks for a transfer of custody.

You keep what happened in clear language. You preserve what matters outside the distortion field. You decide which evidence is needed for legal, financial, or professional reasons and which loops belong only to the injury. You become more interested in anchoring than convincing. More interested in inhabiting truth than winning a debate against someone committed to your diminishment.

This does not mean becoming careless with evidence. Timelines matter. Notes matter. Documents matter. Witnesses matter. Records can protect you. They can also protect your future self from drifting back into the fog. What changes is the emotional arrangement. You stop treating proof as a plea for permission to know what you already know.

That shift brings relief.

The mind begins wasting less life on re-proving, rehashing, defending, and re-entering old courtrooms. Energy returns to invention. To privacy. To work. To desire. To friendship. To the simple dignity of taking up your life without cross-examination.

Boundaries and the Return of Personhood

After coercive control, boundaries can feel uncomfortable. That discomfort carries information. The system trained you to associate limits with cost.

A boundary interrupts reach. It reveals who felt entitled to your availability, your speed, your optimism, your private life, and your future. That is why boundaries so often expose more than they regulate.

You may need boundaries around information, time, body, space, emotion, money, interpretation, access, and expectation. You may need boundaries in the outer world and in your own mind. You may need to stop granting authority to voices that no longer have, or never had, the right to narrate to you. You may need to grieve the relationships, roles, and systems that only felt warm while you were more reachable, more useful, less distinct, and less protected.

That grief is part of the return of personhood.

> *Many people think a boundary has failed if they still feel guilty after setting it, or if the other person objects, ignores it, mocks it, or retaliates. That is old Dead Zone logic.*

A boundary does not become legitimate because the other person approves of it. Approval was never the measure. Protection is the measure. Dignity is the measure. The ability to remain fully yourself without paying a constant tax is the measure.

Sometimes the clearest boundary is a plain sentence. Sometimes the clearest boundary is action without words. A room left. Fewer details. Less access. More privacy. More distance. Shorter contact. No contact. Separate channels. Fewer explanations. No debate.

You do not have to make your boundaries emotionally comfortable for the people who benefited from your lack of them.

That is part of what changes now.

Turning Forward

Regret can become one more undertow if you let it. After coercive control, the mind keeps wanting to turn back toward the reef and study the wreckage from every angle. You replay the sentence you wish you had said, the boundary you wish you had held sooner, the invitation you wish you had declined, the pattern you wish you had named earlier, the moment you wish you had left. Wish feels gentler than blame, but it can keep you facing backward too long. It can still tempt you to believe that if you revisit the old water enough times, you may finally find the version of the past that does not hurt.

But the past does not become safe because you understand it better.

There is a point at which looking back stops being witness and starts becoming another form of self-abandonment. You are no longer gathering truth. You are standing in old surf, asking the sea to return what it already took.

Part of what makes this so hard is that coercive control does not only leave grief. It leaves rejection. It leaves demoralization. You do not only mourn what was lost. You feel cast out of something you hoped would hold. You feel the insult of having offered love, loyalty, labor, patience, trust, or devotion, only to be treated as if your humanity carried less weight than the Controller's convenience. That kind of injury can make the mind keep circling. Rejection wants an explanation. Demoralization wants reversal. Both can keep you staring behind you, hoping that one more pass through the wreckage will restore your standing.

It will not.

> *Regret has its place. It can clarify. It can teach you where you went numb, where you overrode yourself, where hope kept you in old weather too long. But regret was never meant to become your permanent residence.*

Neither was rejection. Neither was demoralization. Those are injuries, not identities. They tell you that something in you was wounded. They do not get to decide the direction of your life.

Turning forward is an act of custody.

You do not owe the past endless re-entry. You do not owe every missed sign another hearing. At some point, dignity asks for a different discipline. Less rehashing. Less bargaining with what has already happened. More willingness to let what was true remain true without revisiting it for one more verdict.

You are allowed to feel rejected without letting rejection define your life. You are allowed to grieve the bond, the fantasy, the future, the version of home or love or belonging you thought was being built.

You are allowed to stop combing the wreckage for the version of yourself who could have prevented every loss. What exists is you now, with more language, more pattern recognition, more standards, and more claim to your own life.

The sea behind you may still be rough. Let it be behind you.

Your work now is not to become the perfect historian of your injury. Your work is to become the faithful builder of your future.

Returning to Your Own Chart

Returning to your chart does not mean returning to who you were before the storm as though nothing happened. It means becoming someone whose instruments are back in hand.

You read the weather differently now. You notice the cost sooner. You read minimization faster. You notice where your body tightens. You care more about access. You let fewer people close enough to rearrange your life before trust has been earned. You stop admiring intensity for its own sake. You become harder to capture through fog.

That does not make you closed. It makes you less colonizable.

There is dignity in that. There is freedom in that. There is relief in that.

Your chart returns one reading at a time. One refusal at a time. One cleaner record. One sturdier standard. One boundary held through discomfort. One old story no longer believed. One private truth no longer surrendered for the sake of ease.

That is how authority comes back.

Not by magic. By custody.

Chapter Eight

Your Life Is Not Up for Negotiation

After coercive control, many people think recovery should begin with clarity. Better understanding. A steadier mind. That makes sense. Reality had to be named. Shame had to be reassigned. The old fog had to be called what it was. But a Stormproof life asks for more than insight. It asks for a return to rightful waters.

Your life is not up for negotiation.

That is not a slogan. It is a course correction.

> *Coercive control does not only wound. It alters the conditions under which a person lives.*

It sends weather into places that should have remained under your own command. Time. Privacy. Work. Rest. Money. Attention. Movement. Desire. Dignity. Not because you offered them up, but because the system kept pressing against your perimeter until too much of your life had to be spent managing the storm.

That is how occupation works. Not usually through one dramatic seizure. Often, through repeated incursions that make the shoreline harder to defend. A little more access here. A little more pressure there. A little more deference dressed up as love, duty, maturity, professionalism, family, or opportunity. Over time, what should have remained protected begins to feel exposed to negotiation, not because it ever rightfully was, but because the weather has been battering the same coast for too long.

This chapter begins with a different premise.

Your life was never meant to be run on those terms.

You were never meant to live as though peace had to be purchased with more of yourself. You were never meant to treat your privacy as suspicious, your needs as excessive, your boundaries as aggression, or your own mind as a territory requiring outside approval. You were never meant to become the breakwater for someone else's storms, ambitions, or profit while calling that love, character, loyalty, or strength.

Recovery asks for more than getting out of the storm. It asks for rebuilding on rightful ground.

That is the deeper shift here. Not becoming invulnerable. Not becoming cold. Becoming stormproof in the truer sense. Building a life whose seawalls hold. Building a harbor in which your personhood is not negotiable cargo. Building terms sturdy enough to reveal when other people's appetites, moods, ambitions, or injuries attempt to redraw your coastline.

A Stormproof life does not begin when you stop feeling pain. It begins when your life stops being arranged as though your humanity were the most flexible thing in the room.

Your life is not up for negotiation.

The rest of this chapter is about what begins to rebuild once that truth is set back on bedrock.

The Border Returns

After coercive control, boundaries can feel charged. That charge gets misread all the time. People think the discomfort means the boundary is too harsh, too selfish, too late, or too much. More often, the discomfort is showing you how thoroughly the old system trained you to associate limits with cost.

A boundary interrupts reach.

That is why coercive systems resent it. A boundary exposes who felt entitled to your permeability. Who was relying on your willingness to absorb the hit, keep the peace, hand over the time, explain again, soften again, stay available again.

In the old regime, your availability may have been treated as the default. Your privacy as negotiable. Your body as easier to claim than to ask for. Your standards were flexible if that flexibility served the system. No wonder the body can react as though a simple limit were an act of aggression. The system trained you to buy calm with access. It trained you to confuse overexposure with intimacy, over-functioning with love, and self-erasure with maturity.

That feeling is old weather.

> *A boundary protects the conditions under which personhood remains livable. It protects your time from occupation. It protects your body from entitlement. It protects your privacy from annexation. It protects your labor from endless requisition.*

It protects your money from being used as leverage. It protects your mind from voices that have lost the right to interpret you. It protects your future from being quietly reorganized by a system you already know too much about.

Many survivors discover that the deepest boundary work begins in the mind. You stop granting interpretive authority to people and systems that used it against you. You stop letting old voices sit in the control tower. You stop treating your own life as open territory.

Sometimes the cleanest boundary is plain language.

I am not available for that.
I will not discuss this by phone.
Email only.
That information is private.
I am leaving now.

I am not continuing this conversation.
That decision is final.
This is mine.
No. This is not acceptable.

Sometimes the clearest boundary is structure. Less access. Fewer details. Longer intervals. Separate channels. Shorter visits. No visits. A lawyer handling contact. A revised routine. Sometimes, the most important boundary is the withdrawal of your inner availability to the old regime. You stop rehearsing arguments for an absent audience. You stop trying to persuade people who lost the right to narrate to you. You stop organizing your choices around anticipated criticism from those who benefited from your smaller life.

That is boundary work too.

Anger That Serves You

Anger can feel disproportionate or embarrassing at first, especially when the person who caused the injury has already moved on, rewritten the story, or found a new supply. That does not make the anger wrong. It means the system trained you to distrust your own protest.

Many survivors fear anger because coercive systems taught them that anger was dangerous when it came from them and permissible when it came from the dominant party.

So, anger goes underground. It becomes fatigue, numbness, self-attack, politeness that costs too much, endless overthinking, and one more measured response to something that should have provoked a harder no.

Healthy anger marks the place where occupation occurred. Anger says this crossed a line. This was not earned. My life is not here for your use. My body is not here for your entitlement.

> *My labor is not here for your convenience. My silence is no longer your cover. My dignity is not negotiable.*

Anger clarifies what shame keeps muddy. Shame turns the blade inward. Anger turns your attention back toward the breach. Shame keeps you auditing your worth. Anger restores proportion.

That does not mean anger should run the whole ship. Anger needs form. It needs enough protection that it does not get lured back into old loops of pleading, proving, or reenlistment. But anger has real work to do in recovery. What matters is what anger serves. If it sharpens standards, protects access, clarifies boundaries, and returns you to your own side, it becomes part of repair. It helps loosen the old arrangement in which your pain had to stay elegant enough for others to tolerate.

Anger can be a valuable fuel to help you return to your own side.

Standards Over Hope

Standards decide what kind of life you are available for.

That matters after coercive control because many survivors emerge with strong feelings and weak terms. They know what hurt. They are less clear on what must now become non-negotiable. The old system trained adaptation. Standards reverse that. They give your life shape before pressure arrives.

A hope says I want better treatment. A standard says this is the minimum condition under which I remain.

Standards can apply to love, work, friendship, family, mentorship, housing, money, sex, privacy, health, rest, and time. They tell you what earns access and what forfeits it. They tell you what kind of leadership you will not work under, what kind of closeness you will not subsidize, what kind of family contact now costs too much, and what kind of charm no longer gets to outrank evidence.

Standards work best when they are grounded in observation rather than panic. They are not there to make you invulnerable. They are there to stop you from calling injury normal.

A standard may sound plain. I do not stay where my reality is repeatedly mishandled. I do not share finances without full transparency. I do not remain where privacy is treated as guilt. I do not preserve contact at the price of self-respect. I do not mistake domination for love, leadership, family, guidance, or opportunity simply because the packaging is polished.

Standards make the future easier to read. They also expose what many people and systems offered only so long as your perimeter stayed weak. That grief belongs here. Standards do not only protect. They reveal. They show which bonds were relying on your reduced selfhood. That hurts. It also clarifies who or what was never safe enough to build around.

Money Stops Serving the Regime

Money is rarely only about money after coercive control. It carries fear, dependence, humiliation, delay, lost years, interrupted work, compromised judgment, and the memory of having fewer exits than you should have had. A bank balance can hold the emotional weight of the whole regime. So can debt. So can lost earning power. So can the first paycheck after rebuilding. So can the simple act of buying something without explanation.

Coercive systems take money sideways. Through interrupted work. Through induced dependence. Through scrutiny. Through unequal access. Through promises that were never formalized. Through shared-future language that left assets elsewhere. Through hidden income, wage theft, under-crediting, unpaid labor, and professional diminishment. Through making one person's income look central and the other person's expendable.

That is why financial recovery is part of dignity.

Money recovery begins with a hard, clarifying question. What must be separated, documented, protected, untangled, rebuilt, or earned differently so that your life stops being easy to invade?

Some survivors need to learn that privacy around money is allowed. Some need to relearn that earning need not be humiliating. Some need to reclaim the right to want stability, comfort, beauty, margin, help, and rest without defending those wants against an old accusing voice.

Money becomes one of the clearest measures of regained freedom when it begins serving your life rather than your reduction.

Work Without Occupation

Work is one of the places where coercive control leaves especially confusing marks.

For some survivors, work became impossible to protect because the relationship, family system, or role consumed too much bandwidth. For others, work was the site of coercion itself. A controlling boss. An exploitative mentor. A punishing team. An institution organized around somebody else's ego. A culture where deference was misnamed professionalism. Some had their ambition used against them. Some had their competence harvested. Some remained in work but lost authorship, confidence, and continuity.

That injury often shows up later as self-doubt. Why can't I focus as I used to? Why do I overprepare, overexplain, brace around authority, underprice myself, freeze when I need to advocate, distrust praise, panic after visibility, or feel strangely tired by opportunities I once would have wanted?

The answer is often that work became linked to exposure.

A Stormproof relationship to work does not require your diminishment to remain. It does not feed on confusion as a management style. Your reality does not become less valid because somebody above you claimed more status.

Your success is not purchased through self-betrayal.

Your skill is not quietly used to build somebody else's monument while your own name grows faint.

For some people, rebuilding work means returning to an interrupted path. For others, it means redefining success after learning how easily status can disguise exploitation. For others, it means choosing a saner scale, slower trust, clearer documentation, less charisma, and more structure.

Work becomes Stormproof when it no longer depends on old coercive bargains.

Freedom in Plain Sight

Freedom often arrives first as contrast. A meal without commentary. A weekend not arranged around someone else's agenda. A room in which you do not need to explain your face, your tone, your body, your fatigue, your silence, your joy, or your no. A workday without manipulation dressed as opportunity. A family interaction that does not leave you diminished for having a self. A schedule that begins feeling like yours again.

These moments can seem small. They are not small. They are evidence.

Freedom after coercive control can feel quiet. More space in the mind. Less interruption. Fewer internal negotiations. A growing unwillingness to call friction normal. More disgust at what used to pass for ordinary.

Freedom also carries grief. Once your standards rise, you see more clearly what the old system costs.

Once you learn what ordinary respect feels like, the earlier injury may sharpen before it softens. Once your own life becomes more inhabitable, you may feel sorrow for how long you lived under narrower terms. That grief belongs to freedom. It means contrast is returning.

Some survivors fear freedom because coercive systems trained them to associate freedom with punishment. If I become too separate, something bad will happen. If I stop carrying this, I will lose love. If I ask for fair terms, I will lose the role. If I tell the truth, I will feel like I don't belong. If I choose for myself, I will become the villain. Those fears can remain active long after the structure has changed. Freedom requires practice, so the body learns a new sequence. I chose. I remained. My life expanded.

That is one way freedom becomes believable again.

Desire Comes Back by Degrees

Coercive control reaches far beyond crisis. It gets into the appetite. It gets into rhythm. It gets into the body's sense of what counts as home.

That is why recovery can feel incomplete even after major decisions have been made. The legal boundary may be set. The breakup may be final. The boss may be gone. The family contact may be reduced. The mentor may no longer have the same access. Yet daily life can still feel flattened from within. Desire may hesitate. Belonging may still feel loaded. Ordinary pleasure may still seem harder to enter than it once did.

That is not small damage. It reaches close to the center of a life.

Desire is often one of the first casualties of coercive control. Desire here means more than sex. It includes appetite for work, beauty, rest, solitude, intimacy, food, friendship, travel, money, movement, style, purpose, joy, and future. It includes the ordinary human capacity to feel drawn toward what enlarges life.

A coercive system taxes desire because desire creates movement, and movement threatens control.

If your wants have repeatedly been criticized, delayed, ignored, mocked, priced too high, sexualized, or reframed as selfishness, disloyalty, distraction, or emotional neediness, desire begins to protect itself by dimming. After enough repetition, people stop reaching not because they lack vitality, but because wanting has become associated with drag, punishment, or humiliation.

Recovery asks for a gentler relationship to desire than many survivors first bring to it. They interrogate desire the way the old system did. Is that too much? Is that realistic? Is that vain? Is that irresponsible? Is that neediness? Is that me being dramatic again?

A better question is simpler. What feels alive here?

That question does not require a dramatic life decision in the moment. It helps you notice where appetite still exists beneath old pressure. These are not indulgences. They are coordinates.

Belonging Without Self-Betrayal

Belonging is one of coercive control's favorite disguises. Many people stay too long because what they are preserving feels larger than the injury. A marriage. A family. A home. A role. A mission. A company. A team. A future. Coercive systems know this. They offer belonging early and then make it conditional later. You may be welcomed as special, central, chosen, one of us. Over time, the terms tighten. Belonging becomes something you keep earning through adaptation.

That is one reason the aftermath hurts so much. The loss is rarely only the person. Often, it is the collapse of the atmosphere in which you believed your place had been secured. It is the pain of knowing how much you compromised yourself to stay.

Belonging under coercive control comes with a hidden surcharge. Contribute, but do not outgrow the rank assigned to you. Be loyal, but do not require too much protection in return. Fit yourself to the family, the role, the leader, the relationship.

That arrangement trains a distorted hunger. Survivors may still crave places that ask them to shrink because shrinking became braided into the old feeling of home. The body can confuse familiarity with safety. A controlling family can still feel like a place of belonging. A difficult boss can still feel like a form of legitimacy. A punishing team can still feel like an identity. A romantic bond can still feel like shelter because desire, fear, and hope were tied together there for so long.

This is why belonging must be rebuilt to be Stormproof.

> *Real belonging does not require chronic self-editing.*
> *It does not treat your dignity as the cost of entry.*

It does not use your longing to keep you available for poor treatment. It does not grant warmth only when you are easier to govern.

Many survivors first encounter healthier belonging in very quiet ways. A group where you are not scanning for correction. A workplace where your competence does not become an invitation to use you up. A home where you can close a door without emotional consequence.

These moments matter because they teach a better standard. Belonging and subordination are not the same thing. Inclusion and occupation are not the same thing. Loyalty and self-erasure are not the same thing.

That distinction could feel uncomfortable, even dangerous, at first if your life taught you otherwise. You may need to grieve the forms of belonging that were never sturdy enough to hold your full humanity. The family that wanted access more than a relationship. The partner who wanted devotion more than mutuality. The boss who wanted contribution more than authorship. Grief belongs here. So does relief.

A more faithful belonging becomes possible when your own reductions are no longer the price of admission.

Daily Rhythm as Repair

Daily rhythm is where recovery becomes visible. Coercive control breaks rhythm. It breaks mornings with dread. Evenings with rumination. Sleep with vigilance. Solitude with guilt. Pleasure with commentary. A person can spend years in a sequence of broken rhythms without naming the degree of injury that creates.

A Stormproof life is built through repeated conditions that make the nervous system less available for occupation.

Waking without immediate dread. Protecting sleep. Protecting work blocks. Letting rest count. Taking a walk without defending it. Having a home rhythm that does not revolve around somebody else's agenda. Having enough margin that joy is not always postponed until after the next emergency. Having rituals that return you to yourself rather than to the old system.

These rhythms may sound modest. They are not modest in their effect.

A life can begin returning through ordinary sequences. Morning light. Coffee or tea in peace. A protected stretch of work. Music that belongs to you. Moving your body because it feels good or is necessary rather than because someone is evaluating it. Phones that can go unanswered. Quiet that does not feel threatening. Bedtime that serves restoration rather than the night watch of old fear.

That is how the body starts learning what the mind is still trying to believe. I have time. I have privacy. I can think. I can move at my own pace. I can want what I want. My life is not currently under occupation.

When Your Life Feels Like Yours Again

All of this belongs together because it answers the same question.

Does your life feel like yours when you are inside it?

That question reaches beyond symptom relief. A person can function and still feel estranged from their own days. A person can achieve and still feel occupied. A person can be admired and still feel lonely in the deepest sense. Coercive control leaves that kind of estrangement behind because it trains you to live in response rather than in authorship.

Recovery asks for a different atmosphere. A life where belonging does not require self-betrayal. A life where rhythm is sturdy enough to protect your body, your mind, your work, your pleasure, and your privacy. A life where rest does not have to be earned through collapse. A life where your preferences carry standing again. A life whose terms no longer make your humanity negotiable.

You do not have to solve all of this at once. Many people first recover these things in fragments. One honest friendship. One less interrupted workday. One meal enjoyed in peace. One standard held. One purchase made without explanation. One choice that does not get run through the old tribunal before you act on it.

These fragments matter.

> *A Stormproof life is built that way. Not through one perfect act of reinvention, but through repeated conditions in which your own humanity stops having to negotiate for its place.*

That is how personhood returns in lived form.
As a structure.
As practice.
As a life less easy to enter, rearrange, and use.

Chapter Nine

The Stormproof Self

By the time you reach this chapter, you may be tempted to imagine recovery as a return to the person you were before coercive control. That longing makes sense. You miss your old ease. Your old certainty. You may want your former self back because that self seems less burdened, less watchful, less marked by the weather you crossed.

Recovery rarely works that way.

The goal is not a perfect restoration of the self who entered the storm. Too much has been learned. A different task is now in front of you. The task is to become someone whose life is harder to colonize.

That is the Stormproof self.

The Stormproof self is not armored to the point of numbness. Stormproof does not mean closed. It means structurally less available to domination. It means your life is built on enough integrity, privacy, standards, self-trust, and practical protection that bad weather has less chance to become your climate.

That distinction matters.

Many survivors fear they must choose between openness and safety. The old system taught them that being open meant being rearranged, used, and interpreted by someone else. So, they imagine strength as hardness and healing as withdrawal. Stormproof expects more than that. It asks for permeability with perimeter. Belonging without surrender.

The Stormproof self still has a heart. The difference is that the heart is no longer running the whole ship with sabotaged instruments.

What the Stormproof Self Knows

The Stormproof self knows that early intensity is not proof of depth.

The Stormproof self knows that relief can be real and still become a route of control. That family language can hide domination. That guidance can become ownership. That discipline can become cruelty. That charisma can coexist with cowardice. That being chosen is not the same thing as being respected. That ambiguity often carries information. That confusion is not always complexity. Sometimes confusion is the product.

The Stormproof self knows that weather belongs on the chart.

A drop in your stomach counts. A pattern counts. A repeated cost counts. A relationship that gets harder to inhabit counts. A workplace that keeps undermining your authority counts. A family contact that always leaves you smaller counts. A team culture that asks your body or conscience to disappear counts.

The old system trained you to override those readings. The Stormproof self takes them seriously much sooner.

That does not make you paranoid. It makes you seaworthy once again.

Self-Trust Returns Differently

Self-trust after coercive control often returns with a different texture than before.

Before, you may have trusted because good faith seemed like the baseline. You expected other people to be limited by your humanity in roughly the same way you were limited by theirs. You expected mutuality, yet it was not performed. You gave the benefit of the doubt as a normal act of relational goodwill.

Now, self-trust may feel less innocent and more grounded. You still know how to hope, but you no longer confuse hope with evidence.

> *You still know how to love, but you no longer hand over authorship.*

You still know how to work, but your competence is not available as a public utility for systems that erode you. You still know how to belong, but you don't mistake self-reduction for intimacy.

This version of self-trust is quieter and stronger.

It knows that discernment is not cruelty. That privacy is not dishonesty. That caution can be loving. That "no" is not a failure of character. That standards are not punishment. That your full humanity is not a negotiable claim.

That is one reason self-trust can feel almost holy in the aftermath. It returns as a reclaimed authority over your own reading.

What Stormproof Does with Love

Stormproof does not ask you to stop loving.

It asks you to stop tolerating occupation.

"Love" under coercive control often became mixed with management, uncertainty, emotional taxation, diminished range, and the hope that enough goodness would finally produce humane terms. Stormproof love moves differently. It does not treat your boundaries as a threat. It does not need your confusion or the other's speed to secure your loyalty.

The Stormproof self learns to ask better questions around love. It continues to ask these questions as due diligence as a regular part of the relationship throughout the years. It is especially important to maintain this discipline throughout the relationship to keep it healthy.

Do I get to exist more fully here? Do I leave contact more coherent or less? Does this closeness widen my life or narrow it? Does this person take my humanity as a limit? Do I feel safer being more real, or safer being less visible? Are care and accountability braided together here, or does one keep replacing the other?

These questions help keep love from becoming another site of amnesia.

What Stormproof Does with Work

Stormproof also changes your relationship to work.

Many survivors emerge from coercive systems with altered instincts regarding ambition, leadership, hierarchy, visibility, and authority. Some become too eager to prove they are not weak. Some become reluctant to be seen at all. Some keep overworking because overperformance once bought temporary safety. Some underprice themselves because the old system trained them to expect under acknowledgment. Some become suspicious of praise. Some remain vulnerable to exploitative sponsorship because specialness still feels like a form of survival.

The Stormproof self does its work differently.

It respects clarity over charisma. Terms over seduction. Structure and documentation over vibes. Mutuality over extraction. It becomes wary of people who enjoy worship and more interested in systems that can tolerate truth, proportion, and shared reality.

Stormproof work lets your skills belong to you again.

Stormproof and Home

Home means more after coercive control because the old system often entered there first.

Home may have been a house where your comfort had less standing than the Controller's priorities. A family where closeness required distortion. A workplace that took over your nervous system so thoroughly it came home with you every night. A team culture that reached into your sleep, your food, your body, your friendships, and your private sense of self. A relationship that looked like shelter until the shelter showed its teeth and the Controller dropped the mask.

That is why the Stormproof self often becomes deeply interested in home, sometimes for the first time in years.

A home after coercive control may begin as a room where you can shut the door without consequence. A schedule that belongs to you. A meal not under commentary. A bed where your body is not on watch. Windows. Books. Work done without interruption. Belonging without surveillance.

Home is one of the places the body relearns that life can be inhabited rather than managed.

The Stormproof self protects that.

The Shape of a Stormproof Life

A Stormproof life is built through choices that reduce the likelihood that coercive weather can quietly become your climate again.

That shape may include boundaries, more privacy, clearer work terms, stronger financial independence, slower trust, calmer homes, better sleep, safer sex, fewer explanations, more documentation, less idealization, more care in choosing who gets close, and more willingness to leave when the old currents begin to reappear.

It may also include pleasure. Beauty. Friendship. Desire. Rest. Art. Nature. Humor. Work that feels alive again. New community. Different rituals. More solitude. More room.

Stormproof is not only defensive. A life spent only trying not to be hurt again remains too organized around the old regime. Stormproof asks for positive architecture.

> *What gives your life buoyancy? What widens reality? What lets your body exhale? What makes you more available to your own future than to your own fear?*

That is part of why coercive control hates a truly recovering person. Recovery withdraws too much labor from the old system. Recovery makes you less convenient for manipulation. Recovery stops offering reverence to structures that fed on your diminishment. Recovery becomes difficult to colonize.

That is a profound change in rank.

The Beacon Is No Longer Outside You

At the beginning, the Beacon may have felt external.

A friend. A screenshot. A note. A body signal. A pattern you could no longer unknow. Something outside the fog that kept telling the truth when your own life had grown too difficult to read cleanly from the inside.

Over time, something shifts.

The Beacon moves inward.

You no longer need as much external confirmation to know when the air has changed. You notice the cost sooner. You recognize diminishment faster. You don't hand your own reading over to systems that previously benefited from your doubt. You trust your standards sooner. You trust your no sooner. You return to yourself faster after contact with bad weather.

That is authorship.

The Beacon was never supposed to remain outside you forever. It was supposed to help guide you back to your own command.

The Stormproof self is what begins to emerge when that return is well underway. More faithful to your reality. Less available for use. More protective of dignity. Less misled by false light. More willing to build a life around what restores range, appetite, privacy, self-respect, and home.

The sea is still the sea. There will still be weather. There will still be charisma, rescue, longing, pressure, beauty, love, grief, ambition, and risk.

> *A Stormproof life does not remove weather from the world. It changes what gets in and stays, what gets mistaken for care, and who holds the chart.*

Chapter Ten

Cast Off! Release the Chains

By now, you know more than you did when you entered this book.

You know that coercive control is not a string of bad moments loosely tied together. You know that it is a system. You know how it enters, how it extracts, how it distorts, how it narrows a life, how it leaves residue, how it converts your strengths into infrastructure for someone else's power, and how it tries to keep its hold long after the visible structure has cracked.

You also know something harder and kinder.

What happened to you did not happen because you were foolish, weak, too trusting, too ambitious, too loving, too emotional, too much, or not enough. What happened to you happened because a coercive system found ways to use your humanity against you. It found your longing, your conscience, your loyalty, your devotion, your capability, your hope, your appetite for love or meaning or excellence or family or belonging, and it converted those qualities into routes of access. That was the injury. Naming it changes the weather.

Fog always served the Controller. Fog kept you explaining away costs that should have counted, defending realities that should have stood, delaying exits that should have been easier, and searching for moral coherence in systems that fed on your confusion.

The Beacon cuts through that.

Early on, the Beacon may have lived outside you. In a document. A note. A witness. A friend. A text thread. A court filing. A pattern that refused to go back underwater once you had seen it.

That is often how it begins.

At first, you need something outside the distortion field to help your mind and body remember that your experience has shape. That your pain has context. That your confusion was not proof against you. That your life was being handled under altered terms. Over time, something changes. The Beacon starts moving inward.

You notice the cost sooner. You notice diminishment sooner. You feel the old weather earlier and believe yourself faster. You recognize false rescue sooner. You lose less time to bait. You stop arguing so long with what your body already knows. You stop asking systems organized around your reduction to certify your humanity.

That is a profound return of custody. The Beacon was never meant to stay outside you forever. It was meant to guide you back to your own chart.

That is the deeper promise of recovery. Not that you become innocent again. Not that you never feel grief, fear, anger, longing, or fatigue again. The promise is that your life becomes less available to occupation. Your standards rejuvenate. Your boundaries hold more quickly. Your work, money, home, privacy, friendships, desire, and rhythms begin serving your life again rather than someone else's primacy.

That is a Stormproof life.

The Beacon Is No Longer Outside You

Stormproof does not mean invulnerable. It means structured. It means your life is built on enough self-trust, enough privacy, and enough material and emotional integrity, so bad weather is less likely to become your climate. It means you are less likely to mistake domination for love, belonging, mentorship, or discipline. It means you know more quickly what costs too much. See *Appendix D* for some case studies of how others have made this journey.

That change may look quiet from the outside.

You leave sooner.
You explain less.
You trust yourself faster.
You let fewer people close without evidence.
You choose work, love, family, friendship, and home on clearer terms.
You become less distracted by false light.
You become more interested in what widens your life, and less tolerant of restriction.

This is how dignity returns in lived form.

You may still miss what you thought was true. You may still carry anger. You may still feel the ache of years lost to fog, to shrinking, to overwork, to fear, to waiting, to trying to earn humane treatment from systems that were not built for it. That grief belongs here. It does not cancel your recovery. It proves the scale of what mattered.

Let it move through. Let it tell the truth. Then keep building.

Build the career, the morning, the income, the friendships, the pleasures, the privacy, the standards, the rhythms, the future, and the love that no longer requires your diminishment.

Build the life that gives your personhood back its full standing.

That life may begin in modest ways. A quieter morning. A day not spent decoding. An hour that belongs only to you. A standard held. A boundary without apology or re-explanation. A walk taken because the weather is beautiful and nobody gets to tax your joy for it. These are not small things.

This is how occupation ends.

You have crossed difficult water. Some of it you crossed alone, even when other people were physically present. Some of it you crossed while doubting your own map. Some of it you crossed while carrying far too much for too long. Some of it you crossed, believing the harbor was real. Some of it you crossed after the harbor revealed itself to be another route of control.

You are here now. The Beacon is no longer outside you. It is yours.

And that changes the voyage.

Context-Specific Screens for Coercive Control

Coercive control does not belong to romance alone. It can take shape in a variety of settings, including work, athletic settings, family systems, or through the slow conditioning of predatory trust capture. The setting changes. The governing logic does not.

These brief screens are meant to help readers notice patterns that can be harder to name when the language of control is disguised as opportunity, excellence, family loyalty, mentorship, or special closeness.

Use the same scale for each screen.

1 = **not at all**
2 = **a little**
3 = **neutral, mixed, or sometimes**
4 = **quite a bit**
5 = **severe, frequent, or very true**

Please add your responses to get a **total score out of 100**.

20 to 39

Lower concern. This does not rule out harm, but the overall pattern is less strongly endorsed here.

40 to 59

Mild to moderate concern. Some coercive or emotionally abusive dynamics may be present and deserve closer attention.

60 to 79

Strong concern. The pattern may be affecting your self-trust, daily freedom, body, functioning, or identity in meaningful ways.

80 to 100

High concern. The pattern is likely severe, pervasive, or life-shaping.

No brief screen can tell the whole story. What matters is not only whether a few moments felt bad. What matters is whether a pattern has begun to narrow your life, weaken your authorship, and make resistance more costly.

Appendix A-1

Are You Being Professionally Controlled, Diminished, or Mentally Occupied?

1. I felt unusually chosen, singled out, or specially recognized in a way that quickly deepened my investment.

2. I feel that access to opportunity, advancement, or legitimacy depends too much on staying in this person's good graces.

3. I am more careful than I should have to be about tone, timing, or disagreement around this person.

4. I often leave interactions with this person second-guessing my judgment, memory, or interpretation.

5. My ideas, labor, or contribution have been used in ways that feel under-credited, appropriated, or structurally unequal.

6. I feel pressure to be unusually available beyond normal professional boundaries.

7. I have begun organizing my work or decisions around this person's moods, preferences, or likely reactions.

8. I feel there are moving standards or hidden rules that make it hard to succeed cleanly.

9. I have been praised in ways that felt exhilarating but also made me more dependent on this person's approval.

10. I worry that resisting, disagreeing, or separating could damage my reputation or future opportunities.

11. I have seen this person revise conversations, decisions, or commitments in ways that leave me doubting my own reading.

12. I feel pushed to accept intrusion or overreach because it is framed as mentorship, leadership, or high standards.

13. I have felt ashamed, diminished, or quietly humiliated at work in ways that made me feel smaller.

14. I feel more isolated than I used to be from independent perspectives, allies, or safe reality checks.

15. I notice myself doing emotional labor to steady this person or prevent fallout.

16. I feel my ambition has become braided with fear.

17. I have tolerated things I would once have questioned because I believed the opportunity or mission was too important to risk.

18. I feel more depleted, less confident, and less professionally solid than I did before this relationship or system.

19. I feel my work life has become narrower, more occupied, or less fully mine.

20. I suspect the problem is not only pressure or difficulty, but a larger pattern of domination, dependency, and control.

Red-flag items: 4, 10, 11, 16, 18, 19, 20.

Appendix A-2

Are You Under Coercive Control in an Athletic or Elite Performance Setting?

1. I felt unusually selected, favored, or specially believed in by a coach, trainer, or program.

2. I feel my place, status, or future depends too heavily on staying in this person's good graces.

3. I am careful about tone, expression, and disagreement because pushback feels risky.

4. I have learned to ignore my own body signals to stay in favor or avoid punishment.

5. My pain, injuries, limits, or fear have been treated as weakness or character failure.

6. I feel pressure to be unusually available beyond what is healthy or reasonable.

7. I organize my decisions around the coach's moods, standards, or likely reactions.

8. Expectations shift in ways that make it hard to feel secure or clear.

9. Praise can feel powerful enough that I keep chasing it even when the environment feels harmful.

10. I worry that resisting could damage my status, playing time, recommendations, or future opportunities.

11. I have seen harm redefined as toughness, discipline, or what excellence requires.

12. I feel I must accept intrusion into my body, schedule, food, sleep, or private life.

13. I have felt humiliated, publicly corrected, or made smaller in front of others.

14. I feel more isolated from independent support or from people who would help me think clearly.

15. I do emotional labor to stay legible, compliant, or less inconvenient to the system.

16. My drive to succeed has become mixed with fear.

17. I have tolerated treatment I would once have questioned because I did not want to lose my future.

18. I feel more depleted, less confident, or less fully myself than before entering this environment.

19. I feel my sport or performance life has become harder to inhabit on my own terms.

20. I suspect the issue is not only intensity or high standards, but a larger pattern of domination and control.

Red-flag items: 4, 5, 10, 11, 16, 18, 20.

Appendix A-3

Are You Living Inside a Narcissistic or Coercively Controlling Family System?

1. I feel I must monitor one or more family members' moods to keep the peace or avoid fallout.

2. I am more careful than I should be about honesty, boundaries, and disagreement in family life.

3. I have felt recruited through duty, guilt, closeness, or the idea that family should come before everything.

4. I have stayed invested because I kept hoping the family would finally become fair, warm, or stable.

5. I feel pressure to explain or defend privacy, independence, or ordinary separateness.

6. I have felt responsible for managing family tension or keeping things from falling apart.

7. I second-guess my own reality because family members revise history or deny what happened.

8. I feel my role in the family is more fixed than my actual self.

9. I feel my time, holidays, or major life decisions are treated as more available to family than they should be.

10. I feel punished when I become more separate, more honest, or less compliant.

11. I have experienced humiliation, contempt, mockery, or rank-lowering in family settings.

12. I have felt ashamed in ways that seem bigger than what I did wrong.

13. I feel children, siblings, or in-laws have been used to lower my standing or make me easier to bypass.

14. I feel I must tolerate things for the sake of "family" that I would not tolerate anywhere else.

15. I feel more isolated from outside support or more hesitant to tell the truth about family dynamics.

16. I notice myself doing emotional labor to keep family members in check or to protect the family's image.

17. I feel there are hidden rules, loyalty tests, or no-win positions that make family life confusing.

18. I feel more depleted, less confident, or less fully myself than I was before these dynamics intensified.

19. I feel my life has become narrower or more governed by the family field than it should be.

20. I suspect the problem is not only family difficulty, but a larger pattern of domination, rank, and coercive control.

Red-flag items: 7, 10, 11, 13, 17, 19, 20.

Appendix A-4

Are You Being Drawn in Through Predatory Trust Capture?

Use this screen when the pattern began with specialness, secrecy, unusual trust, accelerated closeness, or the feeling that you were being gradually prepared to accept more than you would have accepted at the start.

1. I felt unusually seen, understood, or singled out in a way that quickly captured trust.

2. The bond felt special, private, or somehow set apart from ordinary scrutiny early on.

3. I was encouraged to feel that this connection was different from other relationships and should be protected.

4. Boundaries shifted gradually enough that I kept adapting instead of clearly objecting.

5. I was made to feel mature, chosen, loyal, or especially important for tolerating things that made me uneasy.

6. I kept telling myself there had not been one clear enough moment to justify stepping back.

7. Secrecy or privacy around the bond was treated as proof of trust, intimacy, or loyalty.

8. My discomfort was minimized, normalized, or reframed as confusion, oversensitivity, or misunderstanding.

9. I felt pressure to protect the other person's image, privacy, or standing more than my own.

10. I noticed myself becoming easier to reach, influence, or isolate over time.

11. I felt subtly tested to see what I would accept, excuse, or keep quiet about.

12. I worried that naming my discomfort would make me look disloyal, dramatic, or complicit.

13. I have felt ashamed in ways that made it harder to tell the truth about what happened.

14. I second-guess my own reading because the progression was gradual rather than blatant.

15. The relationship or arrangement left me feeling more confused about where the line had been crossed.

16. I feel that my trust was deliberately cultivated before the real terms became visible.

17. I feel my silence or adaptation was later used against me.

18. I feel more depleted, less confident, or less clear than I was before the bond deepened.

19. I feel the relationship occupied more of my mind, loyalty, or identity than it had any right to.

20. I suspect I was not simply drawn in, but slowly prepared, conditioned, or captured.

Red-flag items: 4, 6, 7, 11, 16, 17, 20.

Closing Note

These screens are not meant to flatten different kinds of coercion into the same story. A workplace is not a family. A coach is not a parent. A predatory trust-capture dynamic is not identical to a long-term domestic regime. The settings and consequences differ.

What they can share is a governing logic: narrowing your freedom, increasing your dependence, eroding your self-trust, and making resistance more costly than compliance.

That is the pattern these screens are meant to help you see.

Check Your Bearings™: A Recovery Tracker for Life After Coercive Control

Check Your Bearings™ (CYB™) is a structured, survivor-centered tool designed to help you identify and track the effects of coercive control across the major domains of your life. Its purpose is not to reduce your experience to a score. Its purpose is to make hidden damage more visible so recovery can be more precise and your progress over time easier to see.

Some harm reveals itself slowly. A lower score does not mean a domain was untouched. Some damage becomes clearer only after exit, when adrenaline recedes, contact changes, and more truth comes into view. It is common to recognize the full scale of impact later than you wish you had.

If you need to pause during this tracker and return later, do so. If you need to keep these pages hidden, protect your privacy. The point is not speed. The point is accuracy.

How to use CYB™

The first time you complete **CYB™**, you will rate each item across **BDEN**:

> **B** = Before the coercive relationship or system
> **D** = During the coercive-control period
> **E** = End of the relationship or system, including discard, separation, mediation, litigation, exposure, or terminal escalation
> **N** = Now

That first assessment gives you a fuller map. It helps establish your **baseline** and lets you see not only the extent of the impact, but also what progress you may have already made since the end of the relationship or system. Many survivors are stronger, clearer, or more rebuilt than they feel on the inside. The BDEN view helps make that visible.

After that first assessment, future **CYB™** reviews should use **N only**. In other words, you will rate where you are now each time you return to the tracker, ideally every 12 weeks. This allows you to monitor recovery over time without having to re-enter the full history each time.

For your privacy, keep your earlier **B, D, and E** scores in your own records. Also, the first **N** or "now" score. That way, you can compare them against future **N** scores and see your realignment more clearly over time, without needing to store the full history anywhere, public or digital, unless you choose to.

You may want to make notes beside each domain, or you may prefer to move through the tracker more quickly. Either approach is fine.

An interactive version is at **CoerciveControlRecovery.com**, where you can receive a fuller interpretation of your scores, a more personalized recovery plan, and a way to track your progress every 12 weeks as you move toward a better horizon.

A note on minimization

If you notice yourself wanting to reduce your scores because someone else had it worse, pause there. Comparative suffering is one of a coercive system's favorite disguises. The better question is not whether someone else's storm was worse. The better question is: **what happened to your vessel?**

That is what this tracker is here to help you see more clearly, so you can strengthen what was strained, repair what was damaged, and move forward with better bearings.

Instructions

For each impact item below, rate how severe the impact was at each point in time.

Rating key

0 = not present
1 = slight or occasional impact
2 = moderate impact
3 = significant impact
4 = severe or life-shaping impact

Scoring structure

Section I: CYB™ is an impact tracker. It measures the effects of coercive control on your functioning, selfhood, body, practical life, and social world.

Sections II and III address exposure history and acute risk factors. They should be documented separately and should not be folded into the **CYB™** impact score.

Impact = **effect**
Exposure = **context**
Safety = **risk**

Section I

Check Your Bearings™ (CYB™): A Recovery Tracker for Life After Coercive Control

1. Capture

Attachment Coercion & Trauma Bonding

Impact item	B	D	E	N
Difficulty leaving or detaching even when the harm was clear				
Strength of emotional relief after contact, tenderness, or reassurance from this person				
Persistence of hope for repair or return despite a harmful pattern				
Strength of emotional pull toward this person after trust was damaged				

Subtotal:

Love Bombing / Recruitment Impact

Impact item	B	D	E	N
Impact of unusual early intensity or attention on attachment				
Impact of feeling unusually seen, chosen, or special				
Speed of trust caused by early warmth or devotion				
Influence of early intensity on major choices or commitments				

Subtotal:

Future Faking Impact

Impact item	B	D	E	N
Influence of future promises or implied plans on decisions				
Sacrifice made in reliance on a future that was not honored				
Difficulty judging the present because of hope for a shared future				
Harm caused by collapse of the promised future				

Subtotal:

Relational Over-Responsibility

Impact item	B	D	E	N
Burden of feeling responsible for relationship stability				
Burden of carrying more than one's share of repair, planning, or emotional labor				
Burden of managing the other person's moods or reactions to prevent fallout				
Burden of feeling it was my job to keep things from getting worse				

Subtotal:

2. Selfhood: Identity, Voice, and Reality Erosion

Identity Erosion

Impact item	B	D	E	N
Loss of feeling like myself				
Difficulty recognizing my preferences or standards				
Degree of organizing myself around another person's reactions rather than my own values				
Disconnection from parts of who I used to be				

Subtotal:

Suppression of Voice

Impact item	B	D	E	N
Difficulty speaking plainly				
Degree of self-editing to avoid conflict, backlash, or misunderstanding				
Reduction in saying what I really thought, knew, or wanted				
Sense that silence was safer than direct expression				

Subtotal:

Cognitive Erosion and Reality Distortion

Impact item	B	D	E	N
Loss of confidence in my own reading of events				
Need for outside confirmation to trust my own perceptions				
Difficulty holding a clear sense of what was happening				
Degree of ongoing confusion or self-doubt within the relationship				

Subtotal:

Autonomy and Decision-Making Paralysis

Impact item	B	D	E	N
Difficulty making ordinary decisions				
Degree of hesitation because choices felt risky or likely to backfire				
Loss of confidence in acting on my own judgment				
Reduction in sense of freedom to act independently				

Subtotal:

3. Dirty Bombs: Shame and Cognitive Aftermath

Carried Shame

Impact item	B	D	E	N
Burden of shame that felt bigger than what was truly mine				
Sense of being morally stained by what happened				
Burden of humiliation or contamination after the relationship				
Burden of carrying the moral weight of someone else's actions				

Subtotal:

Internalized Self-Criticism

Impact item	B	D	E	N
Severity of harsh self-talk about what was happening or what happened				
Degree of severe self-judgment as the relationship unfolded				
Burden of feeling I should have handled things better at nearly every turn				
Severity of a punishing inner voice				

Subtotal:

Rumination

Impact item	B	D	E	N
Repetition of mental replay about conversations, decisions, or endings				
Effort spent searching for one better move that might have changed everything				
Pull of returning mentally to what happened even when it was exhausting				
Difficulty stopping replay once it began				

Subtotal:

Self-Blame and Recrimination

Impact item	B	D	E	N
Severity of self-blame for what happened				
Burden of feeling I should have known, seen, left, or acted sooner				
Degree of treating the outcome as proof of my failure				
Degree of turning structural harm into a private indictment of myself				

Subtotal:

Recovery Inhibition and Learned Futility

Impact item	B	D	E	N
Degree of feeling that nothing I did would really help				
Degree of feeling that help, change, or repair was pointless				
Loss of confidence that movement would improve anything				
Reduction in effort because failure or backlash was expected				

Subtotal:

4. Body: Trauma and Bodily Burden

Fear and Hypervigilance

Impact item	B	D	E	N
Degree of staying on alert for shifts in mood, danger, or fallout				
Difficulty relaxing because part of me remained on watch				
Degree to which my body behaved as if it needed to anticipate the next hit				
Severity of ongoing keyed-up or alarmed state				

Subtotal:

Dissociation and Depersonalization

Impact item	B	D	E	N
Degree of feeling detached from myself, my body, or what was happening				
Severity of going numb or blank under stress				
Degree of functioning while feeling absent from my own experience				
Severity of feeling unreal or disconnected in moments of pressure				

Subtotal:

Body and Mood Disruption

Impact item	B	D	E	N
Disruption to sleep, appetite, energy, or mood				
Difficulty regulating my body or emotional state				
Severity of exhaustion, panic, shutdown, or sharp mood shifts under stress				
Loss of physical or emotional steadiness				

Subtotal:

Post-Traumatic Reactivation

Impact item	B	D	E	N
Reactivation of older trauma or survival states				
Sense that the past had been pulled into the present				
Degree to which old wounds felt newly alive under pressure from this relationship				
Severity of responses at the ending that felt larger than the immediate event				

Subtotal:

Sexual and Intimacy Boundary Erosion

Impact item	B	D	E	N
Loss of clarity or stability in sexual or intimacy boundaries				
Degree to which intimacy was shaped by pressure, fear, confusion, or entitlement				
Reduction in freedom to choose, refuse, or define the terms of closeness				
Difficulty experiencing intimacy as fully voluntary				

Subtotal:

5. Dispossession: Material and Functional Erosion

Financial and Resource Erosion

Impact item	B	D	E	N
Damage to financial stability or material security				
Loss of access to resources, protections, or options				
Reduction in ability to support or protect myself materially				
Severity of ongoing financial fallout after the relationship ended				

Subtotal:

Time Colonization and Manufactured Overload

Impact item	B	D	E	N
Loss of sense that my time was my own				
Degree of overload, interruption, or occupation that reduced freedom				
Difficulty thinking, resting, or planning because of demands or crises				
Burden of bandwidth consumed by the system's needs or fallout				

Subtotal:

Occupational and Educational Disruption

Impact item	B	D	E	N
Disruption to work, training, or educational progress				
Loss of momentum, focus, or opportunity because of the relationship				
Reduction in ability to contribute or build a future				
Severity of lasting effects on work or educational path				

Subtotal:

Invisible Labor and Backlog Burden

Impact item	B	D	E	N
Burden of hidden labor that others did not see or count				
Burden of cleanup, administration, or repair work left to me				
Severity of deferred burdens coming due at the ending				
Burden of backlog I had to manage largely alone				

Subtotal:

6. The Social Field: Social, Institutional, and Existential Erosion

Public Role Erosion

Impact item	B	D	E	N
Reduction in confidence or solidity in public or professional roles				
Difficulty occupying my visible role steadily				
Loss of authority, credibility, or continuity in outward life				
Reduction in ability to show up fully in public settings				

Subtotal:

Social Narrative Erosion

Impact item	B	D	E	N
Difficulty having my truth spoken, held, or believed socially				
Degree to which others received a distorted version of events				
Damage to credibility or social standing				
Burden of correcting, defending, or carrying narrative fallout				

Subtotal:

Withdrawal from or Loss of Social Support

Impact item	B	D	E	N
Thinning or fracture of my support system				
Degree of withdrawal from people who might otherwise have supported me				
Difficulty seeking help because of shame, fear, or confusion				
Reduction in access to reliable witnesses or refuges				

Subtotal:

Legal and Institutional Disempowerment

Impact item	B	D	E	N
Degree to which institutions or formal processes felt unequal, unsafe, or turned against me				
Degree of feeling reduced, misread, or outmaneuvered in legal, workplace, or formal settings				
Failure of expected systems of fairness or protection				
Severity of institutional processes deepening the injury rather than relieving it				

Subtotal:

Spiritual and Existential Erosion

Impact item	B	D	E	N
Damage to meaning, hope, or trust in life				
Difficulty feeling that life was coherent or morally inhabitable				
Damage to my sense of goodness, fairness, or larger orientation				
Degree of feeling spiritually or existentially diminished by what happened				

Subtotal:

Parental or Nurturer Identity Erosion

Impact item	B	D	E	N
Damage to confidence as a caretaker, protector, or nurturer				
Reduction in trust in my caring instincts or role				
Loss of stability in my nurturing identity				
Severity of injury to this part of me at the ending				

Subtotal:

Time to score!

Gather the Subtotals

Impact item	B	D	E	N
1. Capture				
2. Selfhood: Identity, Voice, and Reality Erosion				
3. Dirty Bombs: Shame and Cognitive Aftermath				
4. Body: Trauma and Bodily Burden				
5. Dispossession: Material and Functional Erosion				
6. The Social Field: Social, Institutional, and Existential Erosion				

Your CYB™ grand total, by timeframe

Before (B)	During (D)	End (E)	Now (N)

Section II

Exposure and Tactics: Not included in CYB™ impact score.

Instructions

Rate how present each tactic was across time. (During, End, Now).

Rating key

0 = not present
1 = slight or occasional impact
2 = moderate impact
3 = significant impact
4 = severe or life-shaping impact

Exposure / Tactic	D	E	N
Threatened or actual physical violence			
Sexual coercion or force			
Intimidation, menacing behavior, or implied threat			
Stalking, surveillance, or invasive monitoring			
Financial restriction, deprivation, or control			
Isolation from friends, family, or support			
Legal, workplace, or institutional weaponizing			
Smearing, narrative manipulation, or reputational attack			

Most active tactics:

1.

2.

3.

Section III

Safety: Acute Risk Markers. Not included in CYB™ impact score.

Instructions

Rate the severity of the following safety concerns across time.

Rating key

> **0** = not present
> **1** = slight or occasional
> **2** = moderate
> **3** = significant
> **4** = severe or urgent

Safety / Risk Marker	D	E	N
Thoughts that life was not worth continuing			
Urges to disappear, not wake up, or stop existing			
Fear of serious bodily harm			
Fear of being killed			
Fear of escalation if refusal, separation, or exposure occurred			
Feeling unsafe alone with this person			
Feeling unsafe after the relationship or arrangement ended			

Most active current safety concerns:

1.

2.

3.

How to Interpret Your Scores

1. CYB™ Impact Score

Your six clusters and totals

Then, sections 2 and 3 are recorded for context and safety awareness only. They are not included in the CYB™ Impact Score.

2. Context: Exposure and Tactics – What methods were used

3. Safety: Acute Risk Markers – What needs special attention now

What Your CYB™ Score Reveals

Reading your pattern

Once you have scored the domains, do not rush to the total as if one number could explain a system this complicated. First, look for

Ask yourself: Where did coercive control make its strongest landfall? Where did coercive control spread into the body? Work? Money? Sense of reality? Voice? Identity? Future?

Breadth of Impact Score

The number of domains with a 1 or above shows how many areas coercive control encroached upon your life. The number of domains with a 2 shows how many areas had a moderate impact. The number of domains with a 3 or above shows a significant or life-shaping impact.

A note on protective adaptations

You may be tempted to judge some symptoms and consequences as examples of inadequacy. Instead, notice these were protective responses against a sick system. Withdrawal may have been triage. Silence may have been tactical. Reduced work capacity may have been evidence of overload, not laziness or incapacity. Dissociation may have been your way of surviving conditions your body could not safely metabolize in real time. Use the CYB™ to track impact so you can stop mistaking adaptive responses to survive a toxic system as proof of failure.

Common Tactics and Their Hidden Costs

The chapters in this book focus on the structure, cost, and aftermath of coercive control. This appendix offers another companion: a way to study the common tactics that often produce those injuries.

If the main text helps you feel the weather, this section is meant to help you identify the machinery. Many coercive tactics work sideways rather than cleanly. They rely on implication, atmosphere, deniability, rank, and consequence. The message lands in the body and in the target's decision-making, even when the Controller never states the threat in a direct sentence.

Tactics That Work on the Mind

Dirty Bombs and Cognitive Aftermath

Carried Shame

What it means: Carried shame is the burden of feeling morally stained by what someone else did to you.

Common tactics:
- humiliating you, then leaving you to absorb the shame
- treating your pain as proof of your defect
- acting without conscience, then implying your reaction is the real problem
- turning your distress into evidence that you are weak, unstable, or too much

Hidden cost: The injury remains misassigned. The system harms you, and you carry the moral bill.

Fear and Hypervigilance

What it means: Your body learns that missing a signal may cost too much.

Common tactics:
- using silence, mood shifts, and delayed punishment to keep you braced
- making ordinary contact feel potentially costly
- punishing independence enough that scanning becomes rational
- charging the atmosphere without needing open conflict every time

Hidden cost: You become tired, over-alert, and easier to govern through anticipation alone.

Trauma Bonding

What it means: Attachment gets braided together with injury, relief, hope, and fear.

Common tactics
- alternating warmth and pain
- wounding you, then reopening hope just enough to keep the bond active
- becoming the source of both distress and temporary soothing
- keeping reward intermittent so longing stays alive

Hidden cost: You may keep reaching toward what hurt you because relief once came from the same place as the wound.

Love Bombing and Recruitment

What it means: The beginning moves faster than trust has earned.

Common tactics:
- overwhelming you with praise, certainty, or unusual promise
- rushing specialness and emotional investment
- mirroring your hopes or values to lower your guard
- creating a story about the bond that later gets used against your clarity

Hidden cost: You become invested before the structure has been honestly revealed.

Future Faking

What it means: The horizon is used as bait.

Common tactics:
- promising repair, commitment, promotion, or stability that never quite arrives
- keeping something important just ahead of the present pain
- using your hope to extract patience and sacrifice
- moving the line every time you get close

Hidden cost: You spend your present life serving a future that remains useful to them and unreal to you.

Tactics That Narrow the Self

Selfhood and Agency Erosion

Identity Erosion

What it means: You become harder to locate within your own life.

Common tactics
- overriding your preferences until they dim
- making your values secondary to their reactions
- treating parts of your old self as inconvenient or selfish
- rewarding you when you become more manageable

Hidden cost
You may still function while feeling less like yourself.

Loss or Suppression of Voice

What it means: Speech becomes expensive.

Common tactics
- punishing directness with chill, contempt, or distortion
- interrupting or re-narrating what you know
- rewarding silence and penalizing clarity
- training you to hedge, apologize, and self-cancel

Hidden cost: You begin treating your own voice as something that needs permission.

Relational Over-Responsibility

What it means: You become the one tasked with carrying what should have remained shared or theirs.

Common tactics:
- making you the stabilizer of moods, logistics, and repair

- turning your maturity into household, office, or team infrastructure
- assigning you the burden of preventing fallout
- treating your over-functioning as love, loyalty, or character

Hidden cost: You feel tasked where you should have felt met.

Reality Theft

What it means: Your sense of what is real becomes contested territory.

Common tactics
- denying what happened after it happened
- revising sequences, motives, and meanings until your certainty wobbles
- treating your reading as suspicious and theirs as authoritative
- shaping the social story before you have spoken

Hidden cost: You lose time, confidence, and mental energy defending the integrity of your own map.

Autonomy and Decision Paralysis

What it means: Ordinary self-direction becomes harder to inhabit.

Common tactics:
- making routine choices feel risky
- reacting badly enough to independence that hesitation becomes rational
- inserting themselves into decisions that should be yours
- training you to factor their mood into every move

Hidden cost
Your own life stops feeling fully navigable from the inside.

Tactics That Reach the Body

Body, Nervous System, and Intimacy

Body and Mood Disruption

What it means: The body takes in the regime, whether the mind has language yet.

Common tactics

- disrupting sleep through pressure, sexual harassment, fear, conflict, or anticipation
- affecting appetite, energy, libido, digestion, or startle response
- keeping your nervous system in oscillation between alarm and collapse
- charging ordinary life with too much consequence

Hidden cost: What looks personal may be structural. What feels like weakness may be an imposed burden.

Post-Contact Activation

What it means: The old field comes back online fast.

Common tactics

- forced contact, sightings, messages, legal encounters, or shared spaces
- reactivating old fear through mere presence
- making the body respond before thought catches up
- leaving you flooded after what looked minor from the outside

Hidden cost: You may mistake activation for regression.

Sexual and Intimacy Boundary Erosion

What it means: Your body is approached as softer territory than it should be.

Common tactics:
- treating consent as negotiable or costly to refuse
- pressuring, tallying, comparing, or sulking around sexual access
- shaping intimacy around entitlement rather than mutual choice
- making refusal carry emotional or relational consequence

Hidden cost: The body stops feeling fully sovereign.

Physical Intimidation

What it means: The body is taught that resistance may carry physical cost, even when the threat remains implied.

Common tactics:
- standing too close, blocking exits, or following you through space
- looming, pacing, staring, clenching, or charging the room
- slamming doors, striking surfaces, or creating force near you
- refusing to let the interaction end when you are trying to leave

Hidden cost: Your body learns to comply early. Thought narrows. Space stops feeling yours fully.

Tactics That Steal Freedom and Function

Dispossession and Functional Erosion

Financial and Resource Erosion

What it means: Options are thinned by what happens to money, documents, access, and material protections.

Common tactics:
- restricting access to money, paperwork, or accounts
- inducing dependence, then resenting or exploiting it
- interrupting earning power
- reorganizing resources unequally through shared-future language

Hidden cost: Dependence becomes a weapon once engineered.

Mobility Control

What it means: Your freedom of movement is quietly taken over through logistics, documents, access, planning, and over management.

Common tactics:
- controlling reservations, itineraries, routes, or timing
- overplanning far into the future in ways that take custody of your options
- requiring access to travel accounts, booking systems, devices, or passwords
- holding passports, tickets, identification, or other key documents
- making movement feel possible only through their approval or management

Hidden cost: You lose spontaneity, privacy, range, and the ordinary sense that you can direct your own movement.

Time Colonization

What it means: Your day still looks like your day on paper, but less of it belongs to you.

Common tactics:
- crowding your schedule with demands, crises, interruptions, or audits
- using ambiguity and fallout to keep your mind occupied
- making their needs feel more urgent and structurally important than yours
- turning communication into hours of management and repair

Hidden cost: You lose not only hours but also authorship.

Occupational and Educational Disruption

What it means: Work, training, or your path grows harder to protect.

Common tactics:
- derailing momentum, focus, authorship, or continuity
- making your growth secondary or threatening
- exploiting your professional hope while narrowing opportunity
- keeping your path tied to their approval or platform

Hidden cost: The injury can outlast the bond by altering confidence, appetite, and trajectory.

Invisible Labor and Backlog Burden

What it means: You carry the cleanup for damage you did not create alone.

Common tactics:
- leaving repair, administration, or emotional cleanup to you
- benefiting from labor that stays unseen and uncounted
- making your competence absorb the mess
- moving on while the backlog remains on your side

Hidden cost: You remain overworked by a system that already took too much.

Tactics That Use Family, Work, and Systems Against You

Social Field and Institutional Harm

Social Narrative Erosion

What it means: Your standing in the larger story gets quietly weakened.

Common tactics:
- circulating distorted versions of you before you can speak
- framing you as unstable, difficult, disloyal, or unreliable
- pre-shaping how others interpret your reactions
- preserving their complexity while flattening yours

Hidden cost: Your truth becomes harder to hold socially.

Legal and Institutional Disempowerment

What it means: Expected systems of fairness become extensions of the original asymmetry.

Common tactics:
- manipulating courts, HR, boards, schools, or mediators through polish, status, or distortion
- using process as a weapon
- benefiting from institutions that underestimate coercion
- leaving you disadvantaged inside systems you expected would protect you

Hidden cost: The injury spreads into trust itself.

Immigration and Residency Status Abuse

What it means: Relocation, sponsorship, residency, citizenship, or unfamiliarity with a new legal environment is used to increase your vulnerability and reduce your leverage.

Common tactics:
- promising help with residency, citizenship, sponsorship, or legal status, then failing to follow through
- encouraging relocation, then withholding support, unhousing you, making entry conditional, or locking you out after dependence deepens
- isolating you from laws, norms, language, rights, and systems you know how to navigate
- using your unfamiliarity with the new setting as leverage

Hidden cost: The move that was supposed to enlarge life becomes another way your options are narrowed.

Family-Hierarchy Humiliation

What it means: Your standing in the household is publicly lowered, often in front of children or family witnesses.

Common tactics:
- correcting, dismissing, or overruling you in front of the children
- allowing children to mock, bypass, or disrespect you without interruption
- siding with children to display your lower standing
- breaking agreements at your expense in family settings

Hidden cost: The home learns the rank order. Your authority becomes easier to bypass.

Using the Children to Lower the Other Adult's Standing

What it means: The language of protecting the children is used to make one adult more governable.

Common tactics:
- invoking the children as the reason your needs do not matter
- framing your wish for respect or boundaries as anti-child
- using the children's preferences as the final authority when it sidelines you
- rewarding children's alliance with the Controller

Hidden cost: You may feel demoted in your own home while being told the demotion is moral.

In-Law Undermining and Family-Field Rank Enforcement

What it means: Your place in the family becomes discussable, degradable, and open to collective handling.

Common tactics:
- allowing in-laws to complain about you as though your character is open for review
- permitting relatives to discuss your suitability, worth, or place
- failing to interrupt smear, disrespect, or humiliation
- allowing in-laws to dominate you in your own home

Hidden cost: You begin to feel outnumbered, scrutinized, and demoted within the wider family system.

Blackmail Through Shame, Secrets, or Unflattering Information

What it means: Your privacy becomes a pressure point.

Common tactics:
- reminding you what they know about your past, body, fears, disclosures, sex life, finances, or mistakes during conflict
- hinting that disclosure or exposure may follow noncompliance
- holding embarrassing material in reserve
- using selective truth to weaken your standing without making a fully direct threat

Hidden cost: Self-censorship grows. Your world narrows. You become less visible. Shame deepens. Privacy stops feeling secure.

Career, Reputation, and Livelihood Threats

What it means: Your future is made to feel more fragile than theirs.

Common tactics:
- making opportunity, credit, and advancement feel contingent on compliance
- signaling who has influence and how much power they hold over your path
- subtly revising your image as difficult, unstable, dishonest, or disloyal
- withholding access, endorsement, support, or visibility after pushback

Hidden cost: Ambition gets braided to fear. Confidence decreases. The future starts feeling safer when it is smaller.

Closing Note

You do not need every one of these tactics for coercive control to be real. One system may lean heavily on intimacy, another on rank, another on children, family, work, money, movement, legal status, or institutional force. The combinations vary. The governing logic does not.

The point of this appendix is not to make you a perfect diagnostician, nor is it an exhaustive list of all the endless ways coercive control can be applied. The point is to help you recognize the pattern more clearly, assign the burden more accurately, and avoid calling injury by softer names than it deserves.

Case Studies

Many want to know what the recovery process looks like. In this section, we will have the opportunity to follow two case studies in detail. In the first case study, a female is in a personal relationship. In the second, we follow a male in a coercive family system.

First Case Study

17 months after Lockout & Discard

Today is a 4 out of 10 day.

She tells me at our coaching session that this is a "4 out of 10" day.

Ten means she feels steady and glad to be here. One means the floor has dropped out. Four means she is upright, functioning, and not especially convincing about it.

Months earlier, this 60-year-old woman was locked out of the home she had been told was hers. No warning. No real conversation. Just a brutal change in weather after years of partnership, shared family life, and the dismantling of a bookkeeping business she had once built well. She had been persuaded to let it go because her domestic partner felt they did not need the money and convinced the woman to let go of her business as a testament of loyalty, because the future was supposedly shared, and because the family was meant to stay together. Later, she learned that the promises she had charted her life by had never been secured in the ways she was led to believe.

Now she is in a studio apartment, wrestling with a shower curtain, driving a rental car, and trying to rebuild her bookkeeping practice after years away from it. Many of her referral sources have found other people to work with, have moved out of the area, or aged out of the need for her services. But she is rebuilding, one client at a time, as she did in her twenties.

That is one version of recovery. Not a triumphant montage. Not a woman rising in immaculate light with a cleaner third act. A client meeting. A shower curtain. Bills. Panic moving through the body like squall weather. The humiliating smallness of a life after it has been stripped down by somebody else's deception.

On this same day, she had already met with clients and helped them bring order to what had been scattered. Other people call her strong, resilient, tough. She can feel those qualities in herself. She can also feel fear. Fear that the former partner will retaliate again. Fear that whatever she builds can still be knocked sideways. Fear that she will never fully stop missing what she thought they had, or who she thought he was.

That is part of the insult of coercive control. You can know better and still grieve the counterfeit.

On days like this, the mind wants to turn backward. It wants to review the fraud, the lockout, the promises, the property, the years, and the cost. It wants to ask why she is even bothering to rebuild now. One answer is obvious. There are bills to pay.

The deeper answer is that if she is going to stay in the story, she refuses to let terror keep its hand on the helm.

So, she notices what is still beautiful. Butterflies moving over flowers. A heron standing in the water. She lets herself imagine old friends, good people, steadier harbors. She tells herself this is just one frame in the reel, not the whole film. She imagines a future version of her life that is larger than this one, not because fantasy solves anything, but because direction matters. The impossible has already happened. That means the future is still open water.

A painful day is still a day. A 4 out of 10 day is still part of a life. Sometimes the rebuild is nothing more glamorous than meeting the client, fixing the shower curtain, paying the bill, noticing the bird, and refusing to let the last bad years become the final authority on what comes next.

You do not need to feel fearless, or even always happy, to keep building.

You need enough ground beneath you to set the next stone, and enough horizon to keep moving toward.

24 Months Later

Today is a 7 out of 10 day.

That matters. Not because seven is triumph, and not because the sea has gone flat, but because seven means the weather is no longer running the whole coast.

Two years after the lockout, she has rebuilt her bookkeeping business to about sixty percent of what it was before the relationship. That may not sound dramatic enough for people who like their recovery stories with a soaring soundtrack and a revenge body. It feels substantial to her. It is honest work. It is income she can trust. It is authorship returning in lived form.

She is still in the studio apartment. To her surprise, she has come to like the lock-and-leave life. There is not much to fuss over in four hundred square feet. At times, its smallness has felt humiliating. Lately, it has felt more clarifying. There is less room for illusion, less room for deferred maintenance, less room for a whole counterfeit life to keep sprawling across the floor pretending to be security.

She goes out more now. Partly because there is not much to do in a small rental. Partly because life has begun to call her outward again. She has reconnected with old friends who were willing to welcome her back after years of capitulating to her former partner's insistence that they always do everything together, usually with his family or his business circle. The old arrangement had a way of making togetherness sound like intimacy when it was often a form of enclosure.

Recently, she met a client at a restaurant across the street from an expensive place where her former partner used to take her to brunch in the last year they were together. It hurt, briefly, to remember how easily he had moved on after nine years and all the pledges she had mistaken for permanence. That pain still comes. What is different now is scale. It no longer floods the whole harbor. It passes through, then passes on.

She said the movie reel of her life now has many more pleasant frames in it than the last years of the relationship.

That is not a small sentence. It means the film has changed directors.

She is living on a lean budget, and she finds that much more dignifying than a supposedly "secure" life with resentment and control threaded through every day. There is less money now and more air. Less square footage and more actual room. Less performance and more peace. The old life had elegance on the surface, but too much of it was financed by distortion, dependency, and the steady pressure of someone else's will. She would rather live in a smaller harbor that is truly hers than in a grand house where the tide was always being pulled by someone else's moon.

Seven out of ten is not the end of the story. It is something better than that. It is proof that a life can become more inhabitable before it becomes easy. It is proof that dignity can return before abundance does. It is proof that the reel can hold more light again, even after years of bad weather.

Second Case Study

The Family Business of Keeping Him in Place

By thirty-eight, he had spent so many years being told who he was in the family that it had started to feel less like a role and more like weather.

He was the reliable one. The one who could take a hit. The one who could be corrected, drafted, burdened, and sent back in. His older sister was the golden child. She could do almost nothing and still somehow count as doing enough. In the family business, she was paid the same as he was, even though she showed up a fraction of the time. She could run personal bills through the company credit card, leaving him scrambling to clean them up. Equality on paper. Extraction in practice.

The system had started early. In middle school, when his grades slipped, his father made him stand in the cold October waters of Lake Michigan as punishment. His sister had been held back a year in school without anything close to the same consequence. That was the family logic in miniature. One child was hardened. The other was protected. One learned that love arrived braided in an ordeal. The other learned that the system would bend around her.

Later, the parents made them co-CEOs of the family's profitable property management company. He carried the operational load while the old rank system kept humming underneath the org chart. His sister's irresponsibility did not disqualify her. It became one more thing he was expected to absorb.

When his father died of a heart attack, his mother informed him that he was now the man of the family. It was not an honor. It was conscription. His mother would withhold his paychecks without notice for perceived slights. He was to steady the business, carry the weight, and keep the structure standing while she moved into what she called early retirement. Retirement, unfortunately, did not include giving up control. She still kept office hours. She still inserted herself into decisions. She still undermined him whenever he tried to lead.

Twice, when he tried to leave for other work, the mother announced that she was dying again.

Some rare cancer. Some grave treatment. Some crisis that would be serious enough to govern him, vague enough to keep him off balance, and private enough that he was not actually allowed into the medical details. He just needed to come back. Needed to resume duty. Needed to forgo his own opportunities in the service of a family emergency that always seemed to ripen the moment separation became possible.

> *That is how some coercive family systems work. Not only through domination, but through perfectly timed fragility. The illness may be real, exaggerated, manipulated, or strategically deployed. The effect is the same. Guilt does the heavy lifting. The adult child gets reeled back in.*

By the third manufactured crisis, something in him had shifted. He had children of his own now.

> *Their needs made the old arrangement look less noble and more predatory.*

He needed a steadier income. He needed a life that did not depend on whether his mother was suddenly ill, abandoned, or in peril the moment he stepped toward freedom. He needed terms that did not require him to remain the family's designated shock absorber.

So, he left.

Not because the system admitted what it was. Not because justice arrived. Not because the golden child suddenly carried her share or the mother surrendered the script. He left because he could no longer afford, financially or psychologically, to keep living inside a structure that called exploitation duty and called endurance love.

That is one of the harder truths for adult children from coercive family systems. The exit rarely comes with a clean verdict. The system does not gather itself and apologize for misassigning the burden. Usually, the person who leaves is still cast as the one who failed the family.

That does not make it true.

Sometimes, the most adult thing a person can do is refuse to remain in the structure that keeps everyone else from feeling the cost.

References

Amber, K. (2026, April 14). *The Quicksand Model®: Why abuse and violence need a new framework*. End Coercive Control USA. https://endcoercivecontrolusa.com/blog-coercive-control-framework/

Bancroft, L. (2003). *Why does he do that?: Inside the minds of angry and controlling men*. Berkley Books.

Biderman, A. D. (1957). Communist attempts to elicit false confessions from Air Force prisoners of war. *Bulletin of the New York Academy of Medicine, 33*, 616–625.

Dutton, M. A., & Goodman, L. A. (2005). Coercion in intimate partner violence: Toward a new conceptualization. *Sex Roles, 52*(11–12), 743–756.

Fontes, L. A. (2015). *Invisible chains: Overcoming coercive control in your intimate relationship*. Guilford Press.

Freyd, J. J. (1997). Violations of power, adaptive blindness, and betrayal trauma theory. *Feminism & Psychology, 7*(1), 22–32.

Harsey, S. J., Zurbriggen, E. L., & Freyd, J. J. (2017). Perpetrator responses to victim confrontation: DARVO and victim self-blame. *Journal of Aggression, Maltreatment & Trauma, 26*(6), 644–663.

Jones, A. R., & Schechter, S. (1993). *When love goes wrong: What to do when you can't do anything right*. Harper Perennial.

Salerno, P. (2025). *Cruelty by nature: The science of intentional abuse*. Peter Salerno.

Stark, E. (2007). *Coercive control: The entrapment of women in personal life*. Oxford University Press.

Acknowledgments

No book on coercive control is written alone. It is shaped by the labor of survivors, advocates, clinicians, researchers, educators, and truth-tellers who keep refusing to minimize invisible harm. I am grateful to be in their company.

My deep thanks to **Sue Bookchin** for her insight and activism at **Be The Peace Institute**. Thank you for creating more space in the world for healing and clarity. To **Morna**, thank you for your brave advocacy. To **Karen**, thank you for bearing witness and lending human dignity to so many. To **Lisa Fontes, PhD**, thank you for your pioneering work on coercive control and psychological abuse. Your writing and advocacy have helped countless survivors find language for what happened to them, and this book is indebted to that path-making. To **CarolAnn Peterson, PhD**, thank you for your thought leadership and generous presence along the way. There are many more who have contributed but must remain anonymous, and I'm doubly grateful for their selfless dedication to this work.

And to every survivor who has had the courage to name the weather, protect the beacon, and begin again under better terms: this book is for you.

This book is meant as a brief overview and companion, by no means an exhaustive summary of the many dedicated professionals, organizations, advocates, and trusted friends available to those recovering from coercive control. Every survivor's story is different, and each person's needs, circumstances, and timing are unique.

For more individualized support, you are warmly invited to visit CoerciveControlRecovery.com for coercive control recovery resources, trauma-informed coaching, and consulting. Porter's work is grounded, respectful, and attentive to the complexity of rebuilding after coercive control in intimate, family, and professional contexts, offering steadier support for those who may need a more tailored path forward.